Herbal medicine in primary care

Sue Eldin MSc, MIBiol, CBiol, Dip Phyt, MCPP, MNIMH, FRES
Practitioner of Herbal Medicine, Wapping Health Centre, London, UK

and

Andrew Dunford MB, BS, MRCOG, MNIMH
General Practitioner, London, UK
GP Lecturer at St Bartholemew's & The Royal London School of
Medicine and Dentistry, UK

BUTTERWORTH
HEINEMANN

OXFORD AUCKLAND BOSTON JOHANNESBURG MELBOURNE NEW DELHI

Butterworth-Heinemann
Linacre House, Jordan Hill, Oxford OX2 8DP
225 Wildwood Avenue, Woburn, MA 01801-2041
A division of Reed Educational and Professional Publishing Ltd

A member of the Reed Elsevier plc group

First published 1999
Reprinted 2000

British Library Cataloguing in Publication Data
A catalogue record for this book is available from the British Library

Library of Congress Cataloguing in Publication Data
A catalogue record for this book is available from the Library of Congress

ISBN 0 7506 4053 7

Typeset by Bath Typesetting
Printed and bound in Great Britain by MPG Books Ltd, Bodmin, Cornwall

Herbal medicine in primary care

Books are to be returned on or before
the last date below.

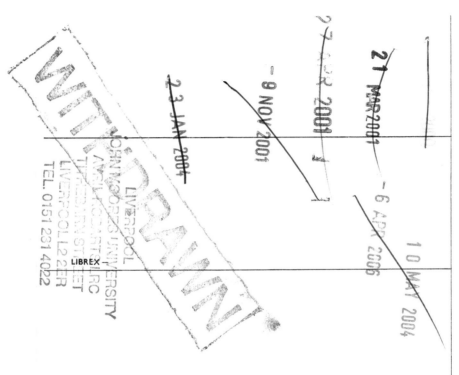

2 1 MAR 2001

2? ??? 2001

- 9 NOV 2001

2 3 JAN 2004

1 0 MAY 2004

- 6 APR 2006

Contents

Preface

Written in 1930 by W. T. Fernie, the following extract from *Herbalism: an Exact Science* perfectly describes the contemporary situation regarding the neglected yet invaluable resource of herbal medicine: it may well have been written today.

Hitherto, medicinal herbs have come down to us from early times as possessing only a traditional value, and as exercising merely empirical effects. Their selection has been commended solely by a shrewd discernment, and by the practice of successive centuries. But today a closer analysis in the laboratory and the skilled provings by experts have resolved the plants into their component parts, both singly and collectively. So the study and practice of curative British herbs may now take rank as an exact science.

This book is dedicated to all previous generations of herbalists who have strived to promote herbalism as an exact science. It certainly has an important role in modern medicine.

Acknowledgments

We wish to thank Miss Margery Whalebone for donating an 1884 edition of the *British Pharmacopoeia*, and for the loan of the pestle and mortar for the front cover illustration. Thanks are also due to Mr Leslie Smith for preparing two of the Figures, and to Christina Lott for reading through the proofs. The encouragement and interest of the staff and patients at Wapping Health Centre is warmly acknowledged. The two cartoons are reproduced by permission of Punch Ltd.

Introduction

This book has been written in order to provide an up-to-date account of western herbal medicine (phytotherapy) for doctors and other healthcare professionals who are interested in the scientific aspects of its theory and practice. It does not set out to provide yet another detailed text on herbal medicine: rather, it aims to present succinctly those aspects of herbal medicine that are of particular relevance to healthcare professionals in order that they may be able to inform accurately those patients who increasingly request this form of 'alternative' treatment.

The topics chosen for consideration are those which are most frequently asked about by colleagues and patients at the health centre, and are therefore not restricted to topics that are purely herbal in context: the inclusion of aspects of pathology and allopathic therapeutics is deliberate. This reflects the fact that a herbalist working in a NHS health centre must be as familiar with the allopathic approach as with the herbal management in order to allow meaningful discussion with the GPs and other members of the primary healthcare team. However, it is also hoped that this book may be of interest to herbalists in that they may gain valuable insight as to what it is like to work within the NHS. The presence of a medical herbalist in a NHS health centre increases the therapeutic repertoire of the centre and exposes the GPs to first-hand experience of treatment using 'alternative' medicine. Understandably, unless allopathic practitioners are directly involved with herbal medicine on a day-to-day basis, they perceive and propagate a very inaccurate picture of herbal medicine. At Wapping there is a strong symbiosis between the GPs and the medical herbalist, each gaining from the other's specialist skills.

As will be seen, herbal medicine lies very comfortably alongside orthodox medical practice. At Wapping Health Centre, patients have had access to herbal medicine since 1991, and they are able to consult a medical herbalist on the NHS. It is the experience of working within such a unique environment, together with the feedback from patients, that has been the main inspiration for this book. As busy practitioners themselves, the authors well recognize that their readership requires essential aspects rather than a detailed consideration: however, for those that are inspired to find out more, there is a reference section at the end of each chapter.

1
What is herbal medicine?

Phytotherapy can be defined as the study and application of the therapeutic effects of plant materials within an holistic context. However, before presenting a detailed consideration of phytotherapy, it is first important to dispel some common misconceptions and to make it clear what western herbal medicine is **not**.

Phytotherapy is not homoeopathy

Herbal medicine is completely different from homoeopathy, although it is commonly confused with the latter. This is probably because homoeopathy also utilizes herbs, and products from both disciplines are routinely available over-the-counter in virtually every pharmacy. It is assumed that purchasers are fully familiar with the vastly different principles behind these forms of treatment, which is rarely the case.

Approximately 65 per cent of homoeopathic medicines are derived from plant material (Kayne, 1997), so they are by no means exclusively herbal. They may also comprise material of animal origin (e.g. extracts from the poison sac of *Apis mellifica* – the honeybee) or minerals (e.g. sulphur). It was Samuel Hahnemann (1755–1843) who first instituted and formalized the system that forms the basis of modern homoeopathic practice. Interestingly, it was his dissatisfaction with the current accepted practice of the eighteenth century that caused him to abandon orthodox medicine and its overuse of substances that he considered highly toxic. It was his brief encounter with herbal medicine as he worked on a German translation of Cullen's *Materia Medica* that was to result in his formulating basic homoeopathic principles. Hahnemann was particularly interested in the use of cinchona bark to treat malaria; he found that, by taking an extract of the bark, he developed some of the symptoms of malaria. From this experience he developed the idea that a substance capable of producing the symptoms of a disease could also be used to treat that disease, but only if administered in very small doses.

The basic homoeopathic principle that Hahnemann went on to develop can be summarized as the selection of a remedy which, if given to a healthy individual, will produce a range of symptoms similar to those observed in the afflicted patient. This was described as 'proving'. Hence the most important principle of homoeopathy, *similia similibus* (like cures like). At the core of the treatment is the second principle; the administration of minute quantities of the chosen remedy in order to avoid toxicity. As will be seen, it is this difference in posology that forms a major departure from herbal medicine. The final principle was that only one remedy should be used at any one time; nowadays, however, it is common for practitioners to prescribe more than one substance. These three rules form the basis of classical homoeopathy. Another important distinction between herbal medicine and homoeopathy concerns the actual form of the medications. The whole basis of homoeopathic treatment relies on the use of tinctures prepared by serial dilutions of the original 'mother tincture'. It is this repeated dilution of the original material that causes most problems in attempting to explain, in scientific terms, how the resulting medicine can work, since at dilutions greater than 10^{-23} (with reference to Avogadro's Law) there can be no molecules of the original substance in solution. Potencies commonly utilized today include dilutions of 10^{-12}, 10^{-24}, 10^{-60} and 10^{-200}. As can be appreciated, this has been the cause of much scepticism in orthodox medical circles, as well as the subject of much research within homoeopathy itself. Experiments carried out by Benveniste (Davenas *et al.*, 1988) purported to demonstrate that ultra-high dilutions of IgE antiserum would stimulate *in vitro* degranulation of human basophils. This set of experiments gave rise to great debate, and they were eventually investigated and found to be flawed (Maddox *et al.*, 1988). A repeat of the original work failed to gain the same results (Hirst *et al.*, 1993). Meanwhile, Benveniste continues to research this aspect of homoeopathy (Benveniste, 1998). The best-known general explanation of how such very high dilutions of a substance might exert an effect relates to what is described as the 'memory of water'. A detailed consideration of this is beyond the scope of this book, but Endler and Schulte (1994) have researched it extensively.

The above paragraph briefly summarizes the main features of the theory of homoeopathic treatment, in order that the most important differences between the latter and herbal medicine can be fully appreciated. Of more direct relevance to the patients is the actual difference in the form of the medications.

The standard tinctures used in herbal medicine are quite different from those of homoeopathy. Firstly, they are prepared by steeping

Figure 1.1. *Little girl:* 'Please, sir, I want the hundredth-thousandth part of a grain of magnesia.'
Young chemist: 'Very sorry, miss, but we don't sell in such large quantities.'

the plant material in alcohol, and the final product is not usually diluted; thus they are concentrated, highly potent preparations, and are usually taken as the unmodified liquid tincture (see Chapter 5). The observed physiological effect is directly due to the chemical constituents derived from the plant material. In addition to this main form of preparation, individual herbalists will also prescribe other types of medicine – for example, lotions and creams for topical application. Many also advocate the use of fresh herbs for the preparation of teas, etc. The range of medications will be considered in Chapter 5. In homoeopathic practice it is common to be prescribed medication in tablet form; however, this is not the case in herbal medicine. About 5 per cent of the herbal prescriptions at this Health Centre are for tablets, and they are prescribed only when the constituents of the plant are such that they are not extracted well in alcohol due to their low solubility in this solvent – this applies to those herbs that are high in mucilages. Thus, the patient consulting a herbalist is most likely to come away with a prescription for a liquid, alcohol-based medication. More often than not, this comes as a surprise to the patient; to date, their only contact with 'herbal medicine' may have been little more than the local health food shop, where the majority of herbal medications are in tablet form. This of course only adds to the confusion regarding the difference between herbal medicine and homoeopathy. In allopathic medicine, the prescription of a liquid preparation is relatively rare, and is restricted to items such as cough medicines and paediatric preparations.

Sceptics find homoeopathy easy to dismiss solely on the basis of the extreme dilutions of the preparations. Even in Victorian times, it was the subject of many a joke (Fig. 1.1). The same prejudice cannot be applied to herbal medicine, since the strong tinctures are easy to analyse, and several of the plants used are the original sources of commonly prescribed drugs. Even so, homoeopathy, which is a relatively new science, is generally better accepted by GPs, many of whom hold dual qualifications. Its link with the Royal Family is probably one of the main reasons for its popularity and recognition. Western herbal medicine, with its ancient history, remains relatively little known.

Phytotherapy is not Chinese herbal medicine

Phytotherapy is not the same as Chinese herbal medicine, which is just one aspect of traditional Chinese medicine. The latter has been firmly established for at least 2000 years, and views disease as the result of a disturbance to the natural environment of the body; the usual homeostatic processes have been overwhelmed, and are consequently unable to restore the harmony and balance of a healthy individual. These are seen as being maintained by an uninterrupted flow of Qi (vitality) through distinct channels of the body. This is superimposed on the theoretical system of Yin and Yang and the five phases. The system is very complex, and it is impossible to do it justice here. However, the main principle is that, in a healthy individual, the Yin and Yang aspects are in balance, although in a constant state of flux. A person who is ill shows either predominately Yin or Yang symptoms, since these two components are no longer in balance. It is the object of the practitioner, via the administration of herbs, acupuncture, massage or other means, to restore the balance.

It is therefore important to reiterate that the use of herbs is a small part of the distinct philosophy that characterizes traditional Chinese medicine. Considering the herbs themselves, the prescription is in a different form to that prescribed by a phytotherapist; the Chinese herbalist usually provides patients with a specially selected mixture of dried herbs, which they then have to make into a liquid (aqueous) extract at home. With the exception of teas, in western herbal medicine it is generally the case that the tinctures (alcoholic extracts) are 'ready-made' and are simply added to a very small volume of water to make them more palatable (see Chapter 5). It should also be noted that the herbs used are different species to those used within phytotherapy – there is a totally different *materia medica*. Nevertheless, it is important to note that several herbs used in the practice of western herbal medicine originated in China (e.g. *Glycyrrhiza glabra* – liquorice). However, they are now being used in a different philosophical framework, which clearly distinguishes the two approaches to treatment.

It is therefore not good enough to call any discipline of complementary medicine 'herbal medicine' simply on the basis that it involves some kind of plant material. Phytotherapy, homoeopathy, and Chinese herbal medicine are all completely separate disciplines.

What is a medical herbalist?

Most people would probably provide a very uncertain answer to this question. Medical herbalists are a rare species, and as such do not regularly come into contact with the general public. One of the places they occasionally feature in is crime fiction, and perhaps one of the best-known herbalists is Ellis Peters' Brother Cadfael. Set in medieval times, *Cadfael* is a popular television series that frequently shows examples of Brother Cadfael's treatment based on his herbal remedies. With the exception of this series, herbalists are not seen as central characters. In Agatha Christie stories, for example, they are usually depicted as eccentrics who spend their time in panelled libraries examining samples of dried herbs. They are then called in by one of the main characters to solve a poisoning case. Recently, an episode of a major TV series centred on a coroner's office featured a self-poisoning case. In one scene, the main characters were to be found surrounded by piles of herbals, eagerly researching the identity of a plant rhizome implicated in the poisoning. A medical herbalist was nowhere to be seen. The very idea that such a specialist could be consulted is still novel. However, phytotherapists are a new generation of scientists and, within the next decade, their specialist skills will undoubtedly be routinely acknowledged.

This book seeks to illustrate how a medical herbalist, consulting with a primary healthcare team, can provide valuable information on appropriate treatment plans. The old-fashioned image is being dispelled, and a medical herbalist is now just as likely to be found in a health centre as in a museum library. The future is very exciting; given the right surroundings, herbal and allopathic medicine could support each other and contribute to a holistic health service. Other complementary therapies could similarly be incorporated. The front-line healthcare professionals, i.e. GPs, would soon learn to recognize which conditions respond best to treatment by herbal medicine (and other disciplines), thus optimizing limited funds. The treatment would be far more streamlined, and the oscillation of patients between the various GPs, hospital departments and other specialists would decrease. With the exception of those chronic conditions requiring regular assessment, patients would progress through one course of treatment and, having completed the course, would be unlikely to return. This is not an unrealistic approach, but it relies on a complete reappraisal of the efficacy of the complementary therapies in general, and the removal of the stubborn assumption that allopathic medicine has no room for alternatives. At Wapping, western herbal medicine is alive and well within an orthodox setting.

Wapping Health Centre

Wapping Health Centre is a large inner city practice operating from purpose-built premises. There are approximately 7500 registered patients, with a total of 25 000 GP consultations per annum. It is unusual in that there is high mobility; 40 per cent of the patient population move out of the area every year, and they are replaced to within 100 of the previous total. The local population exhibits considerable ethnic diversity, with a total of 40 different languages spoken. There are three main components: the endemic East Enders, the now well-established Bangladeshi community, and those (who tend to be more temporary residents) inhabiting the Thames-side wharf conversions. With the exception of the latter category, it is largely an impoverished community. Housing is poor, and 40 per cent of children live in non-earning households, with approximately one-third bringing in a total income of less than £4500 per annum. Educational achievement is often very poor, with unemployment reaching 25 per cent amongst those under twenty-five years of age. The death rate is 14 per cent above the national average, and the illness rate 27 per cent higher. Mental illness accounts for 28 per cent of hospital inpatient stays, and this, together with heart disease, is the top cause of ill health amongst the local population (East London Health Authority, 1998). This presents a challenging and exciting environment for a medical herbalist, with many opportunities for health education, especially with respect to diet.

References

Benveniste, J. (1988). Meta-analysis of homoeopathy trials. *Lancet*, **351**, 367.

Davenas, E. *et al.* (1988). Human basophil degranulation triggered by very dilute antiserum against IgE. *Nature*, **333**, 816–18.

East London Health Authority (1998). *Health Action Zone Newsletter*, 1 May 1998.

Endler, P. C. and Schulte, J. (eds) (1994). Ultra high dilution. In *Physiology and Physics* (P. C. Endler and J. Schulte, eds). Kluwer Academic Publishers.

Hirst, S. J., Hayes, N. A., Burridge J. *et al.* (1993). Human basophil degradation is not triggered by very dilute antiserum against IgE. *Nature*, **366**, 525–8.

Kayne, S. B. (1997). Homoeopathic Pharmacy. *An Introduction and Handbook*. Churchill Livingstone.

Maddox, J., Randi, J. and Stewart, W. W. (1988). 'High dilution' experiments, a delusion. *Nature*, **334**, 287–90.

Suggested reading

Barnes, J. (1998). Homoeopathy. *Pharm. J.*, **260**, 492–7.

2

Herbal medicine past and present

> The problem with us scientists today is that we learn no history, so we think that the mental giants of today are smarter than anyone who lived in the past.
>
> *D. Suzuki, 1998*

Herbal medicine is as ancient as the history of mankind, with well-researched records. In a book of this nature it is not possible to cover historicity in detail; therefore, this chapter simply provides a concise account of the most important aspects. It also serves to illustrate how plants have, throughout the ages, played a prominent role in the maintenance of good health.

All ancient civilizations have their own historical references to medicinal plants. In the earliest records, herbal medicine is linked with magic and is repeatedly viewed as being a 'gift from the gods', allowing the people to overcome evil powers on earth. Even these early applications of herbs as medicinal agents demonstrate a remarkable understanding of the differing actions of the individual species. As far as written evidence of the use of plants as medicines is concerned, the earliest reference is found in the Chinese *Pen Ts'ao* ('Great Herbal') of Shen Nung, dating back to 2800 BC; here, over 360 species are listed, including *Ephedra sinica* (MA Huang), which is still used today. Within allopathic medicine, this herb is the source of ephedrine.

Ancient papyri show that in Egypt, from about 2000 BC onwards, there were a large number of physicians who routinely used plants as medicines. They regarded disease as a result of natural causes rather than due to the work of evil spirits. It would appear that it was the ancient Egyptians who first attempted to remove the magical element from the practice of herbal medicine. The Ebers Papyrus, dating from about 1500 BC, mentions specific formulae for named conditions, and the species listed include some that medical herbalists still use today – such as elderflower (*Sambucus nigra*), wormwood (*Artemisia absinthium*) and myrrh (*Commiphora molmol*).

In the earliest Greek records, there are many references to

Asclepiadiae and *Rhizotomoki*. The first group is named after the Greek god of medicine, Aesculapius, and the second group describes the 'root gatherers' – herb suppliers who were probably one of the first groups of people to make accurate lists of the medicinal properties of the herbs they traded in. The earliest known herbal (dating back to the fourth century BC) is the *Rhizotomika*, compiled by Diocles, who was a pupil of Aristotle. This text contains detailed notes about the herbs' physiological effects.

Dioscorides (*c.* AD 40–80) is a very important figure in the history of herbal medicine; he was a practising doctor who set out to compile a comprehensive herbal showing the characteristics of all the common medicinal herbs as well as their uses. Dating back to the first century AD, *De Materia Medica* (On Medicines) was the first manual of its kind. It was a very detailed text describing about 600 species; it not only provided information on suggested dosages of the various herbs, but also considered possible toxic effects. There was a section on the harvesting and storage of herbs, and advice on how to detect adulteration. Thus, the danger of toxicity was fully appreciated by these early herbalists. Dioscorides had travelled widely as an army surgeon and, as Roman armies travelled around Europe, so their knowledge of medicinal plants accompanied them. Physic gardens were established close to their encampments and, in this way, the Romans effectively spread unfamiliar plants as well as knowledge of their medicinal properties. Two highly favoured herbs were mustard and garlic, which were used in huge quantities, not only for culinary purposes but also to clear infections (garlic) or make poultices (mustard).

The most important figure in the whole history of medicine was Hippocrates (468–377 BC). Often described as the 'father of medicine', he was perhaps the true instigator of holistic treatment. He stressed the importance of keeping detailed case histories, and he firmly believed in treating his patients as individuals. He devised a regime of herbal treatment, using a range of over 400 species. In addition to the herbal medicines, he employed exercise and special diets, each of which was varied to suit the patient's particular symptoms, and was known as his concept of physis. This individual approach is the hallmark of today's herbal medicine. Hippocrates saw disease as the disturbance of the natural harmony of a healthy individual, so his treatment plan was aimed at restoring the balance of what he described as the four 'humours'. These were described in the Humoral theory of Empedocles, a Sicilian philosopher (500–430 BC). He stated that everything was formed from four elements: earth, fire, air and water. These had the associated characteristics of dryness, warmth, coldness and wetness. He then derived the concept of the four humours (fluids): black bile, blood, yellow bile, and phlegm. Each of these humours also had a particular temperament associated with it – namely, melancholic, sanguine, choleric, and phlegmatic. The melancholic temperament was described as 'cold and dry', and illnesses associated with this included depression and constipation. The treatment consisted of administering 'hot' herbs such as *Cassia senna* (senna) in order to decrease the excess of black bile, and so restore the balance. The phlegmatic temperament was characterized by an excess of 'cold and damp', causing conditions such as excessive production of catarrh and resultant chest infections. Herbs that were warm and drying, such as *Thymus vulgaris* (thyme), were indicated. A sanguine temperament resulted from an excess of 'hot and damp', and was characterized by a tendency to over-indulgence. Disorders associated with this category included gout and diarrhoea, and were relieved by herbs which were cooling and drying in nature, for example *Arctium lappa* (burdock). The temperament resulting from an excess of yellow bile was described as choleric, and was 'hot and dry'. It was characterized by hot-tempered behaviour and liver disease. Cool, moist plants such as *Taraxacum officinale* (dandelion) were administered. When all the four humours were in balance, the individual enjoyed good health. This was what Empedocles called a state of crasis; when it was disturbed, a dyscrasia resulted.

In contrast to the relatively flexible and variable treatment plans of Hippocrates was the rigid system devised by Galen (AD 121–180). It was based on the four humours of Hippocrates in that it involved a formal classification of all the medicinal herbs on the basis of how each one interacted with each humour. Thus, each herb was designated a specific 'temperament' (or temperature): hot, cold, moist, dry or temperate. Within these categories, a plant could be in the first, second, third or fourth degree. All physicians were now instructed in the Galen tradition, and the more holistic approach of Hippocrates was, for the time being, developed no further.

There are several others of the Galen period who contributed to the development of herbal medicine, and the reader is directed to Barbara Griggs' excellent book *Green Pharmacy* for further details. In Europe, herbal knowledge was kept alive throughout the Dark Ages (fifth to eleventh centuries) by scribes, and a large number of mainly Greek herbals were collected together in libraries of the rapidly-growing Arab empire. In Baghdad, a team of ninth century translators began the enormous task of translating the works of Galen, Dioscorides, Hippocrates and several other authors. Galen was particularly popular amongst the Arabs, and the works of Rhazes (865–925) embraced his ideas. One of his works includes the comment 'Where a cure can be obtained by diet use no drugs, and avoid complex remedies when simple ones will suffice'. This is very much the therapeutic approach of today's medical herbalist. Avicenna (930–1036), a skilled physician and pharmacist, closely followed the doctrines of Galen and Hippocrates and restated the importance of the four humours in his major work *A Canon on Medicine*.

In general, Galenism continued to be the main approach as, from the eighth century onwards, Greek ideas were translated into Arabic. Three hundred years later these works were translated into Latin and, from the ninth to the twelfth centuries, these translations allowed Arabic contributions to find their way into western thinking. With these ideas came new, exotic herbs such as nutmeg and camphor. It was during this period that the science of pharmacy was being established; very precise formulations for the preparation of medicines are to be found in several of the Arabic manuscripts dating from this period. During the Dark Ages, pharmacy became intertwined with superstition. Several 'Leech Books' (Anglo-Saxon *laece*, to heal) from the period illustrate this, the most famous being the *Leech Book of Bald*. The author was a contemporary of Alfred the Great, and the book is the oldest surviving Anglo-Saxon volume referring to herbal medicines. Bald's therapeutic approach is truly holistic; he not only provides details on the actual medicines, but also full notes on how to approach the patient during treatment. Diet is considered, and suitable foods for various ailments are listed. However, amongst the various healing recipes are those described as being protective against elves and goblins. Another highly organized system of herbal medicine was that developed by the Welsh Myddfai from the sixth century onwards. Truly holistic in approach, it related back to Hippocratic principles: 'Whoever shall eat or drink more or less than he should, or shall sleep more or less, or shall labour more or less from idleness or hardship (being obliged to over exert himself), or who, used to being bled, refrains from doing so, without doubt he shall not escape sickness' (Abithel, 1891). The Myddfai physicians provided a highly integrated system of care until well into the eighteenth century, and most of their infusions were administered as simples (single species), prepared from fresh herbs collected locally.

From about the tenth century onwards monasteries were the centres of medical training and practice, although eventually the Church Councils (1131–1212) prevented the monks offering medical treatment. However, the monastery libraries became the repositories of large collections of reference books on herbal medicine. A large number of works were produced, including *De Viribus Herbarum* by the Bishop of Meung, where the medicinal properties of over 80 plants are described in Latin verse. The *Antidotarium*, written by Nicolaus of Salerno, was a very extensive piece of work, which essentially summarized all the work on herbal medicine carried out at the School of Medicine at Salerno. During the thirteenth and fourteenth centuries, Salerno became the centre of learning for pharmacy.

Much attention was focused on the quality of medicines and, in the thirteenth century, the Catalan Arnau de Vilanova (*c*.1235–1311) gave detailed consideration to this subject. He wrote:

> In the preparation of a medicine, the physician must consider, in order, the cleansing, grinding, measurement, softening and mixing. He should give instructions to his assistants, the apothecaries, about its mixing, telling them when it is to be prepared, lest lacking instructions they make it up later than they should.

He also showed concern regarding accurate identification:

> As for the medicine itself, the physician should reflect on whether he can recognize it or not, and if he can, he should ask to see it and judge it for himself. But if he is not acquainted with it he should consider whether it has been described by the wise, and if so, when he has seen the plant he should decide whether it corresponds to its description and, if so, choose it: while if it does not fit, he should not use it but should choose something generally familiar and fitting the descriptions of the wise.

The above formed the basis of a lecture that de Vilanova gave to students studying the applications of herbs as medicines, and it goes on to give named examples of misidentifications. He considered precisely how different plants should be administered, and which countries provided the best quality plant products, such as ginger and figs. He also showed recognition of the fact that plants grown in different habitats will contain differing amounts of the active principle.

The Middle Ages saw a period when many exotic plant species were introduced – for example, nutmeg and cloves. This was essentially a drawing together of eastern and western medicine. The fifteenth century saw the publication of *De Proprietatibus Rerum* by the Englishman Bartholomew Anglicus (1495). It is historically important, as it contains the first printed botanical illustration.

Many new medicines were being introduced, based mainly on the work of Paracelsus (1493–1541). He was a controversial character, best known for his challenging of medical authority. In 1527 he published a work that questioned the doctrine of humours, and vowed to seek a general reform in medical practice. This did not endear him to his colleagues, who had earlier invited him to be municipal physician in Basle. With this position went the privilege of a lectureship at the University; an opportunity to spread his new ideas. He had a special interest in chemistry, and is credited with the first detailed search for the active principles in medicinal plants. Paracelsus was also a proponent of the use of chemicals (i.e. 'drugs') to treat disease. He argued that such agents were required because disease originated from external influences, and thus required strong chemical substances to counteract them.

Paracelsus' interest in chemistry extended to his promoting the use of herbs in the form of spirits, cordials and waters, which he considered to be highly effective forms of medicines. From the end of the sixteenth century onwards there was a surge of interest in the formulation of recipes for mixtures of health-giving herbs, most containing between 20 and 30 species. Owing to their relatively high cost, use of these was mainly restricted to physicians themselves or to the upper social classes. Distilled medicines became available, and enthusiasm for such preparations did not decline until the early eighteenth century – when John Quincy (1719) dared to suggest that several of the formulations in the current *London Pharmacopoeia* were 'good for nothing', and 'used only by the ignorant'.

Paracelsus undoubtedly succeeded in introducing an investigative edge to medicine in general although superstitions still abounded. For example, the doctrine of signatures (which linked the shape, form or colour of plant structures with their medicinal properties) was still popular. Therefore, a bright yellow plant may have been considered useful in treating jaundice, and those with leaves similar in shape to a particular body organ would be used to treat that organ. Since the spotted leaves of *Pulmonaria officinalis* (lungwort) looked like a diseased lung, this species was used to treat lung disorders. Fortunately for patients, many of these herbs had highly beneficial effects and, in many cases, their chosen application was spot-on in terms of the plant's biochemical constituents.

The Middle Ages also saw the establishment of several universities. Prior to this, medical training was akin to an apprenticeship; the student would develop and extend the ideas of a mentor. University teaching introduced a broad-based, more scientific approach, abandoning many of the classical theories. The centre of university teaching appears to have been in Italy; the University of Padua was established in 1222. The founder of the Royal College of Physicians, Thomas Linacre (*c.* 1460–1524), studied at Padua, returning to Britain in the early 1490s to establish lectureships at Oxford and Cambridge.

The sixteenth century was an exceptionally active period, and in 1542 *De Historia Stirpium* (The History of Plants) by Leonhard Fuch was published. Fuch drew all the plants from nature and, in doing so, established the trend for all future botany texts. Previously illustrations had tended to be copied from other books, and it was common for inaccuracies to be introduced and exaggerated each time they were copied. There are many recorded examples of misidentification of plants resulting from such errors. William Turner's *A New Herball*, dating from 1551, contains warnings about false identifications, even extending to species sold by apothecaries.

In general, this period saw a massive growth in interest in herbal medicines, which was undoubtedly stimulated by explorations into the New World that yielded yet more new plants. It is evident from contemporary Aztec manuscripts, for example the herbal written by Martin de la Cruz (1552), that there was an exceptionally rich flora awaiting investigation. However, very little was written in Europe about such plants, so they remained relatively unknown. One example of a work recording some of these discoveries is John Frampton's 1577 translation of Monardes' work entitled *Joyfull Newes out of the New Founde Worlde*.

The use of New World remedies was not met with such enthusiasm by everyone, and this is reflected by the title of Timothie Bright's work, *A Treatise Wherein is Declared the Sufficiencie of English Medicines* (1580). Here it is stressed that the New World species are more suitable for local diseases. This was a commonly held belief at the time, and reflects the tradition that folk medicine had always relied on fresh, locally grown herbs. Apart from this consideration, newly imported species were very expensive and were available only in the dried form.

The teaching of medicinal botany became more formalized and, in the sixteenth century, botanic gardens were set up at key learning centres such as Padua (1545) and Leyden (1587). The wonderfully titled *The English Physician, or An Astrologo-Physical Discourse of the Vulgar Herbs of this Nation being a Compleat Method of Physick whereby a Man may Preserve his Body in Health or Cure himself being Sick, for Three Pence Charge, with Such Things one-ly Grow in England, they being Most Fit for English Bodies*, by Culpepper (1653), is another well-known volume. He was deeply disliked by other physicians because he dared to translate the *London Pharmacopoeia* from Latin into English, thus allowing other apothecaries to understand it and thereby enabling them to treat the poor, who were otherwise unable to obtain expensive medical treatment. Culpepper pays particular attention to the English herbs, rather than the more exotic varieties from abroad, as indicated in the above extensive title of his text! Unfortunately he also reintroduced a magical element into herbal medicine through linking it with astrology, just as herbal medicine was acquiring a more scientific edge.

Although not directly linked with the evolution of herbal medicine, Andreas Vesalius' book *De Humani Corporis Fabrica* (The Structure of the Human Body), dating from 1543, cannot be ignored. It added greatly to knowledge of how the human body functioned, and therefore contributed to the evolution of medicine in general. Like Fuch's work, all the illustrations were drawn from nature, and it was thus a major publication on human anatomy.

William Harvey (1578–1657) was also active during this period, and he was one of the first true scientific investigators of human anatomy and physiology. He worked out the circulation of blood, albeit not the precise relationship between the blood in arteries and that in veins, although he did acknowledge that such a link must exist. It was Malpighi (1628–1694) who filled in the gap after observing capillaries under the microscope.

For the greater parts of the seventeenth and eighteenth centuries it would appear that herbal medicine was somewhat in decline as the upper classes continued to experiment with 'modern medicine', which included exciting, if rather dangerous, substances such as arsenic and mercury. Blood-letting was also very popular as a 'cure all'; even William Harvey, with his analytical approach to the study of anatomy and physiology, was a proponent of this popular form of treatment and stated that it was 'foremost among all general remedies'. Just as he found it hard to abandon such well-established forms of treatment, he also found it difficult to drop the pre-Copernicus theories of astronomy that had long since been superseded.

Eventually there had to be a departure from the use of such unsafe practices as blood-letting and the administration of toxic emetics. In North America, Samuel Thomson (1769–1843) attempted to consider afresh the cause of disease and concluded that it resulted from a disturbance of the four elements within the body – i.e. earth, air, fire and water. This is reminiscent of Hippocrates' four humours. Thomson had an extremely narrow view of what caused disease; namely, a blockage or interruption in the normal channels of dissipation of heat. The body's normal responses to a raised temperature include increased sweating so, during conditions which resulted in fever, he would administer strong diaphoretics such as capsicum in order to strengthen the body's own normal reactions. Predictably, Thomson was dismissed by contemporary practitioners as no more than a quack; however, they could not ignore the fact

50   BRITISH PHARMACOPŒIA.

exhibits about fifteen vittæ. They have an agreeable aromatic odour, and a sweetish spicy taste.

Preparations.

Aqua Anisi | Oleum Anisi

ANISI STELLATI FRUCTUS.
Star-Anise Fruit.

The dried fruit of Illicium anisatum, *Linn.*; *Nees, Plant. Med.* plate 371. From plants cultivated in China.

Characters.—Star-anise fruit is usually composed of eight fully developed carpels diverging horizontally in a stellate manner from a short central generally stalked axis. Each carpel is boat-shaped, more or less beaked, irregularly wrinkled, of a rusty-brown colour, and commonly split on its upper margin so as to expose its solitary flattish smooth shining somewhat oblique reddish-brown seed. Odour and taste of both pericarp and seed closely resembling anise fruit.

Preparation.—Oleum Anisi.

ANTHEMIDIS FLORES.
Chamomile Flowers.

The dried single and double flower-heads or capitula of Anthemis nobilis, *Linn.*; *Bentl. and Trim. Med. Pl.* vol. iii. plate 154. From cultivated plants.

Characters.—The single chamomile flowers of commerce are those in which the capitula have some yellow tubular florets in the centre, surrounded by a variable number of those which are white and ligulate; the double flowers are those in which all or nearly all the florets are white and ligulate. In both kinds the receptacle is solid, conical, and densely covered with chaffy scales; and both varieties, but especially the single, have a strong aromatic odour and very bitter taste.

Preparations.

Extractum Anthemidis
Infusum Anthemidis . ½ ounce to 10 fluid ounces
Oleum Anthemidis

ANTIMONII OXIDUM.

Oxide of Antimony.

$$Sb_2O_3.$$

Take of
Solution of Chloride of Antimony . 16 fluid ounces
Carbonate of Sodium . . . 6 ounces
Water . . . . . . 2 gallons
Distilled Water . . . . a sufficiency

Pour the antimonial solution into the water, mix thoroughly, let the precipitate settle, remove the supernatant liquid by a siphon, add one gallon of distilled water, agitate well, let the precipitate subside, again withdraw the fluid, and repeat the processes of affusion of distilled water, agitation, and subsidence. Add now the carbonate of sodium previously dissolved in two pints of distilled water, leave them in contact for half an hour, stirring frequently, collect the deposit on a calico filter, and wash with boiling distilled water until the washings cease to give a precipitate with a solution of nitrate of silver acidulated by nitric acid. Lastly, dry the product at a temperature not exceeding 212° F. (100° C.)

Characters and Tests.—A greyish-white powder, fusible at a low red heat, insoluble in water, but readily dissolved by hydrochloric acid. The solution, dropped into distilled water, gives a white deposit, at once changed to orange by sulphuretted hydrogen. It dissolves entirely when boiled with an excess of the acid tartrate of potassium.

Dose.—1 to 4 grains.

Figure 2.1. Extract from 1884 edition of the *British Pharmacopoeia*.

that patients preferred his approach to treatment, leading to an undercurrent of interest in herbal medicine being shown by several leading orthodox practitioners. Local Indian traditional herbal medicine was being extensively investigated, and some practitioners began to take an interest in the herbs that were used.

Dr Wooster Beach (1794–1868) was keen to restructure the practice of mainstream medicine, but certainly not by developing Thomson's untrained simplistic approach. He proceeded to introduce 'botanic medicine' into his own practice, which made him very unpopular amongst mainstream practitioners; however, this did not deter him from setting up the 'Reformed Medical Academy', whose training covered the use of local herbs. His attempt to combine a scientific medical approach with a sound knowledge of botany caused his movement to be described as 'the Eclectics'. The hallmark of this form of medicine was that all treatment was designed to 'act in harmony with physiological laws'.

Thomson's approach continued to come under attack, and was described by John Buchanan as a 'bane to society'. It was brought to Britain by Albert Isaiah Coffin in 1838 and, following an unsuccessful start in London, he moved up to the north of England, where herbal medicine was more popular. He organized groups called 'Friendly Botanico-Medical Societies' and distributed the *Botanic Guide to Health*, which offered herbs he had imported from America as well as local species. Once again the popularity of herbal medicine was related to the class structure of that time; those who could not afford orthodox physicians' fees consulted Coffin and his fellow practitioners, and found herbal medicine to be very efficient. Thus, for the time being, its survival was guaranteed.

Dr Beach came over from the United States to promote Eclectic medicine in England, and damned Coffin's system in the same way as he had Thomson's. He even managed to convince a colleague of Coffin's, Skelton, that his system was superior. As a consequence, Skelton now wanted to be counted an Eclectic – the new wave of botanic medicine in Britain. Eventually this brought positive results for herbal medicine, as Skelton managed to combine the more scientific orthodox approach with 'botanical medicine'. Both disciplines began to benefit from modern advances in pharmacy, chemistry, etc. Such a scientific approach would have been condemned out of hand by both Thomson and Coffin.

Following Thomson's death in 1841, Alan Curtis set up the Physio-Medical Institute in the United States, but in turn its practice of using a large number of different herbs in large doses was frowned upon. A time of great change and reform followed; at one time the Eclectics experimented with isolates (i.e. single substances) and were criticized for doing so. During Victorian times the orthodox medical profession dramatically reduced the use of blood-letting, although several toxic drugs were still popular. Leeches were now the preferred agents for 'cleansing' the blood. By the 1890s 'botanic medicine' was undergoing a new revival, and people were routinely using herbal medicines. This is illustrated by the fact that herbal preparations and orthodox medicines appear side by side in editions of the *British Pharmacopoeia* dating from this period (Fig. 2.1). Here in Britain this was not yet the case, but the Eclectics did gradually drop the use of extracted plant substances, and the National Association of Medical Herbalists (established in 1864) continued to battle for further acceptance of herbal medicine.

One of the main reasons for the survival of 'alternative' medical systems such as homoeopathy and herbal medicine is that, during the Victorian era, the main emphasis was on private subscription to support medical institutes such as the Pasteur Institute (established in 1888) and the Robert Koch Institute (established in 1889). There was much rivalry, as indicated by the closeness of the opening dates, and the Lister Institute in Britain followed in 1891. They all date from after the period where the germ theory had been developed, with its promises of protection against various diseases by means of vaccination. Since there was no state-funded system, the poor either paid into their own insurance schemes or paid for the services of local 'alternative' practitioners. Their approach became referred to as 'fringe medicine' by those who were now relying mainly on synthetic chemicals to restore health, rather than methods aimed at supporting the body's own natural healing powers. These forces were originally described by Hippocrates as *vis medicatrix naturae* (the healing power of nature). This effectively rationalized allopathy as the administration of a chemical agent that would restore the balance of health by acting directly against the causative agents of the disease. In some cases the mainstream practitioners remained helpless; for example, they could not find an agent effective against tuberculosis, which was one of the main causes of death in the latter half of the nineteenth century and the early part of the twentieth century. Under these circumstances allopathic doctors were only too happy to resort to the recommendation that patients should spend time abroad in more favourable climates, and thus the richer clientele were sent to the south of France, the Swiss Alps or Egypt. Until the discovery of streptomycin by Selman Waksman in 1940 there was no other realistic approach, although improvement in public and personal hygiene had gone a long way to reduce mortality. There was a resurgence of interest in herbal medicine around the time of the First World War, when supplies of herbs from overseas dwindled

HERBS FOR HEALTH

$\mathfrak{Section}$ $\mathfrak{Seven}$

HERB SIMPLES
PILL SIMPLES
POWDERED HERB SIMPLES

HERB SIMPLES

Simples not mentioned in the following list can almost invariably be supplied by giving the common name of the Herb or its botanical name. We have sources of supply from which we can obtain any well-known Herb.

332 AGRIMONY (*Agrimonia Eupatoria*) — Coughs, diarrhœa, relaxed bowels, kidney and liver derangements.

334 ANGELICA (*Angelica Arch. angelica*) — Stimulating and aromatic. Kidney trouble and producing perspiration.

337 ARRACH (*Chenopodium olidum*)—Hysteria, and purely female complaints. A powerful nerve tonic.

951 ASH LEAVES (*Fraxinus excelsior*)—Useful in case of gout and rheumatoid arthritis.

339 AVENS (*Geum urbanum*)— Astringent, styptic and tonic.

341 BALM (*Melissa officinalis*)— Cooling for fevers. Induces mild perspiration.

343 BALM OF GILEAD (*Populus candicans*)—For affections of the chest, lungs, stomach and kidneys.

345 BALMONY (*Chelone glabra*) —Constipation, dyspepsia, jaundice, for worms in children.

348 BLACKBERRY (*Rubus villosus*)—An excellent tonic. Useful in cases of diarrhœa, etc.

350 BLACK CURRANT (*Ribes nigrum*)—For hoarseness, sore throat, coughs, and catarrh generally.

351 BLADDERWRACK (*Fucus vesiculosus*) — Effective for obesity and for kidney trouble.

352 BLUE MALLOW (*Malva sylvestris*)—Popular for coughs, colds, etc.

355 BONESET (*Eupatorium perfoliatum*)—For fever, catarrh, asthma, etc.

955 BORAGE (*Borago officinalis*) —For fevers and chest trouble.

All the above, price per packet, **9d.** *post free*
Large packet (3 times the former), **1/6** *post free*

SECTION SEVEN

257 BROOKLIME (*Veronica Beccabunga*)—Kidney complaints, scurvy, impure blood.

359 BROOM (*Cytisus scoparius*)—Dropsy and kidney trouble generally.

362 BUCHU (*Barosma betulina*)—For gravel and inflammation of the bladder.

365 BUCKBEAN OR BOG-BEAN (*Menyanthes trifoliata*) Tonic. Useful for liver trouble, scurvy, and skin diseases.

367 BUGLE (*Ajuga reptans*)—Used in hæmorrhages, liver disorders, and consumption.

369 BUGLEWEED (*Lycopus Virginicus*)—Used in coughs and bleeding from lungs.

368 BUGLOSS (*Echium vulgare*)—Relieves inflammatory pains, fevers and nervous affections.

372 BURDOCK (*Arctium Lappa*)—A fine blood purifier, for scurvy and eruptions, and also kidney complaints.

373 BURNET SAXIFRAGE (*Pimpinella Saxifraga*) — A remedy for stomach troubles and flatulency.

374 CALAMINT (*Calamintha officinalis*) — Used for coughs, chest colds, and bronchitis.

376 CARROT, WILD (*Daucus Carota*)—For dropsy, retention and irregularities of urine, gravel and other bladder affections.

379 CATMINT, CATNEP (*Nepeta Cataria*)—Very useful in colds, inducing perspiration.

381 CELANDINE (*Chelidonium majus*)—Used in jaundice, eczema, scrofulous, and other skin diseases.

383 CENTAURY (*Erythræa Centaurium*) — For dyspepsia. Mixed with Barberry Bark for jaundice.

386 CHAMOMILE (*Anthemis nobilis*)—For hysteria and nervousness in women, and a tonic.

957 CHERRY STALKS (*Prunus avium*)—A useful tonic and astringent.

387 CHESTNUT LEAVES (*Castanea vesca*)—Very efficacious in paroxysmal or convulsive coughs and other irritable conditions of respiratory organs.

959 CLARY (*Salvia Sclarea*)—For indigestion. Good eye lotion.

388 CLIVERS OR CLEAVERS (*Galium Aparine*)—Excellent for gravel and other urinary disorders. Also a tonic.

CLOWNSWORT — See No. 553 (Woundwort).

391 COLTSFOOT (*Tussilago Farfara*)—A popular and effective cough remedy. Also the basis of Herbal Smoking Mixture.

393 COMFREY (*Symphytum officinale*)—Highly valued for lung and chest trouble. Used as poultice on obstinate ulcers.

394 COOLWORT (*Tiarella cordifolia*)—Counteracts acidity of the stomach. For urinary troubles and a tonic.

395 CRANESBILL (*Geranium maculatum*)—For cholera and diarrhœa. Also of use for internal intestinal hæmorrhage.

398 CUDWEED OR COTTONWEED (*Gnaphalium uliginosum*)—An excellent treatment for quinsy, as a medicine, gargle, and external poultice.

400 DAMIANA (*Turnera aphrodisiaca*)—Valuable as a tonic in debilitated conditions of the reproductive organs. Also as a tonic to the nervous and physical systems generally.

401 DANDELION (*Taraxacum officinale*)—A laxative and a tonic. Useful in correcting kidney and liver disorders.

965 ELDER LEAVES (*Sambucus nigra*)—Excellent for urinary irregularities and epilepsy.

979 EUPHORBIA (*Euphorbia pilulifera*)—Gives great relief in paroxysmal asthma. For chest affections generally.

All the above, price per packet, **9d.** *post free*
Large packet (3 times the former), **1/6** *post free*

Figure 2.2. Extract from the 1937 booklet *Herbs for Health.*

and were replaced by British crops. The Society of Herbalists was founded by Hilda Leyel in 1927, and it went on to publish *A Modern Herbal* in 1931. Between the wars herbal medicine was very popular with the general population, and several specialist mail order firms offered supplies of herbal remedies. The firm 'Heath and Heather', of St. Albans, is typical. Its illustrated booklet of 1937 describes products aimed at the treatment of named conditions such as constipation, influenza, piles, etc., as well as the supply of herbal simples and culinary herbs (Fig. 2.2).

During the 1939–45 war, herbal medicine flourished. Essential medicines were in short supply because imports from the continent were no longer available, and the solution was to return to the situation prior to the 1914–18 war, when a large number of medicinal plants were home-grown. These were either collected from the wild or cultivated as crops. The Royal Botanic Gardens at Kew were to become the centre of operations; here, staff organized plans for cultivation of the most important medicinal species and also considered which species could be collected from the wild. A collection of medicinal plants was established with help from the National Federation of Women's Institutes (NFWI), and the Boy Scouts issued a booklet to aid the identification of the various species. A special series of cigarette cards produced by the London Cigarette Card Company Limited also provided illustrations to help with identification. In 1941 The Ministry of Health set up a Vegetable Drugs Committee (VDC), the main aim of which was to collect species that would yield essential medicines. The work of the NFWI and the Boy Scouts was greatly expanded, and other societies, such as the Women's Voluntary Services for Civil Defence, became involved. The VDC members included representatives from The Ministry of Agriculture (MAF), The Pharmaceutical Society, the Wholesale Drug Trade Association, and Kew Botanic Gardens. They provided advice on collection, storage and distribution, and this was eventually published by Brome and Schimmer, a botanical drug and spice importer. Records show that very large quantities of some species were being demanded; for example 250 tonnes of *Taraxacum officinale* (dandelion) roots. It soon became evident that, although the project had started by encouraging collection from the wild, these supplies were insufficient to satisfy demand. The VDC advised that, initially, concentration should be on the cultivation of five species: *Digitalis purpurea* (foxglove), *Atropa belladonna* (deadly nightshade), *Aconitum napellus* (aconite), *Datura stramonium* (thornapple) and *Hyoscyamus niger* (henbane). The root of aconite was used to treat nerve and joint pain, whilst sedative and antispasmodic drugs were derived from thornapple, deadly nightshade and henbane. It would appear that the major problem encountered in the production of large quantities of medicinal herbs was the drying stage of preparation. This was of crucial importance since, if plant material is not dried correctly, it will contain considerably less of the active principles. Records show that the Treasury did release several grants to help with this problem. Although home-grown herbs were now being cultivated intensively, it was still necessary to import those species that were either not suited to the climate and edaphic factors or contained significantly less of the pharmacologically active ingredients when compared to crops grown in their native climes. Several species were being imported from India, and there were regular complaints regarding poor quality and adulteration. The Acting Director of Kew, Sir Geoffrey Evans, observed that 'Our investigations have shown all too frequently that substitutes and adulterations for the genuine article are coming into the country, with consequent waste of shipping space and labour'. He suggested that botanists based at Indian universities should check all medicinal material destined for Kew. The problem of adulteration and substitution has been a constant problem throughout the history of herbal medicine. Once this problem had been resolved, the imports of thornapple and henbane from overseas were sufficient to allow Britain to concentrate on the cultivation of foxgloves and deadly nightshade.

In 1942, the VDC ceased to exist and was replaced by the Ministry of Supply, which worked in close association with the Medical Research Council (MRC). This allowed the herb growing to more closely satisfy the actual therapeutic needs as identified by the MRC. A National War Formulary was published, which served to advise doctors on the drugs available and what alternatives to use for those in short supply. The *British Pharmacopoeia* and *British Pharmaceutical Codex* were revised to provide details of restrictions on those essential drugs that were in particularly limited supply. The local collection of herbs by the general population had not been forgotten; the new Ministry of Supply produced a series of booklets entitled *The Herb Collectors' Bulletin*, which gave details on collection, drying and dispatching (Ministry of Supply, 1942). The project ran very smoothly, and some 250 drying sheds were active nationwide. In the four years between 1941 and 1945 an impressive amount of material was collected, including 1524 tonnes of fruits of *Aesculus hippocastanum* (horse chestnut) 'conkers', 147 tonnes of *Urtica dioica* (nettle) leaves and 65 tonnes of *Crataegus oxyacantha* (hawthorn) berries (Hastings, 1996). The total for all the species amounted to 4636 tonnes at a value of £121 250 sterling. In 1945, plans for the new National Health Service were being developed by the Ministry of Health, and there was active discussion on future policy regarding cultivation of plants for medicinal use. It is ironic that 1941, the year that saw a resurgence in interest in growing medicinal plants, was also the year that dealt a major blow for herbal medicine in Britain when the Pharmacy and Medicines Act made the practice of herbal medicine illegal. Even so, the National Association survived throughout this time to become, in 1943, the National Institute of Medical Herbalists. In 1964, a team of leading herbalists joined together to fight the 1941 Act. As a result, Fred Fletcher-Hyde, who was also a member of the newly formed British Herbal Medicine Association, began researching the *British Herbal Pharmacopoeia*. This was an essential condition of the reversal of the 1941 Act. It comprised a collection of monographs of all the herbs prescribed by medical herbalists, and is still a key text for today's practitioners. The 1968 Medicines Act gave herbalists new-found freedom, and the professional training has been expanding and developing ever since.

References

Abithel, J. W. (1891). *The Physicians of Myddvai*. London.
British Pharmacopoeia (1884). Spottiswode.
Griggs, B. (1981). *Green Pharmacy*. Robert Hale.
Hastings, L. (1996). The Botanic Gardens at Kew and the wartime need for medicines. *Pharm. J.,* **257**, 923–7.
Heath and Heather (1939). *The Famous Book of Herbs*. St. Albans.
Ministry of Supply (1942). *The Herb Collectors' Bulletin*.
Suzuki, D. (1998). Gene Genie's new vision, by T. Wakeford. *The Guardian Higher*, December 5.

Suggested reading

Porter, R. (1997). *Medicine: A History of Healing*. Michael O'Mara Books.

3

The consultation

Making an appointment

Patients at Wapping Health Centre make an appointment to see the resident herbalist via one of two pathways. They either request a consultation via their own GP, or they make a self-referral at the reception desk. Patients are also referred by other members of the primary healthcare team. This includes the district nurses, health visitors and practice nurses (Fig. 3.1). For example, when monitoring the progress of young children with eczema, a health visitor may suggest a referral to the herbalist in order to discuss ways of treating the condition that do not involve regular applications of steroid creams. Parents are often concerned about this particular aspect. In consulting the herbalist, an additional opportunity is created in order to discuss aspects of diet and development. It has been found that mothers are only too glad of an opportunity to be able to ask a wide variety of questions regarding their children's health.

Once an appointment has been booked, the patient is contacted and the appointment confirmed; there is usually about 1 month's waiting list, so at present acute conditions cannot be dealt with unless a cancellation slot is made available. In an ideal situation, with appropriate funding, there would be a special clinic set aside for acute consultations, where advice on colds, 'flu and minor infections etc. would be given, and a prescription provided there and then. If this were to happen in a health centre setting, it would provide an ideal opportunity to demonstrate just how effective herbal medicine can be for such conditions, particularly when treating children. With the current rate of growth of public interest in 'natural' remedies for minor illnesses, it would probably be very well attended. A further advantage of this would be that it would release GP slots for more serious cases, and it is possible that GP consultation times could be lengthened.

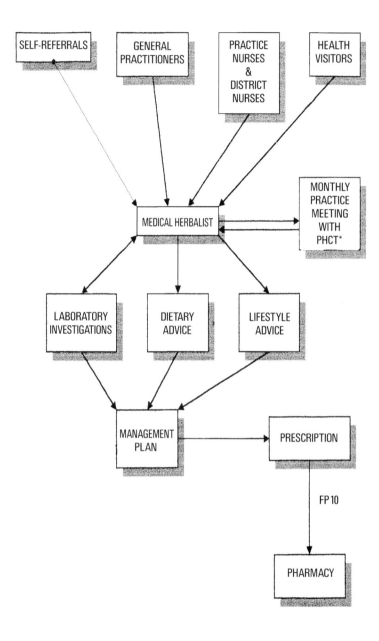

Figure 3.1. Herbal medicine: the integrated approach at Wapping Health Centre.

Meeting the patient

In many respects, a consultation with a medical herbalist is very similar to that with a GP. The physical examination is identical to that carried out by a GP, clinical training being an integral part of the training that a medical herbalist receives. During the initial appointment a full medical history is taken, as well as details of the presenting complaint. In addition, the patient is questioned about the functioning of other body systems that may not necessarily feature in the presenting complaint. Asking such questions may well reveal other symptoms, which could help diagnosis in complex cases. Because so many details are considered, the key feature of the consultation is that at least one hour is spent with the patient at the initial session. However, because each case is unique, there is no set pattern. This is the hallmark of herbal medicine, which employs a highly individual approach to each patient. Thus, in some cases this first hour may be sufficient to consider all the relevant factors – for example, where a patient presents with recurrent cystitis as the major problem. In other cases it may be necessary to book another one-hour session, for example in chronic fatigue syndrome (CFS). The patient is then asked to attend a follow-up session approximately two weeks later. This waiting time is certainly not wasted; the patient is given several things to do, the most important of which is the completion of a diet diary.

The patient patient

Patients consulting a medical herbalist for the first time are not sure what to expect, and it is essential that the practitioner does not make any assumptions regarding their knowledge of herbal medicine. In general, patients are uncertain as to what herbal medicine actually is and, as already pointed out in Chapter 1, a large proportion equate it with homoeopathy. The first step, therefore, is to inform patients, providing an appropriate amount of detail and ensuring that they are not expecting homoeopathic preparations or a bag of dried Chinese herbs to brew up at home. Since the initial consultation is a lengthy one of at least an hour, it is important to gauge this correctly. Many patients are very interested in herbs and will have lots of questions, while others are less interested in the details. The prime purpose of the first consultation is to take a detailed past medical history, so this has to take priority. Even so, it is always made clear that questions are welcome, and a special time at the end of the session can be set aside for this. Patients are often surprised by this, since the average consultation time allocated to a GP doesn't allow for much questioning.

Medicines are never prescribed at the first meeting, in order to allow patients to absorb all the information and complete the diet diary. This ensures that they do not come to regard the herbal medicine as just a different form of 'drug', but rather as part of a detailed holistic approach, which cannot be rushed.

It is important to convey to patients that they have an important role in the healing process. This concept is reinforced by their being given several things to do before their follow-up appointment, including the completion of a diet diary. These activities reinforce their role in getting well, and it may be the first time that they have been encouraged to think in this way. This approach most certainly will not suit anyone who wants instant answers, although this is very rarely the case with those who are chronically ill.

Monitoring progress

Once patients have been assessed by the medical herbalist, their GPs are kept fully informed. There are regular meetings with all the Wapping Health Centre GPs, where their patients' treatment plans are outlined and progress discussed. Much interest in herbal medicine has developed amongst the team, and the number of referrals is constantly increasing as the efficacy of treatment is appreciated and the doctors become aware of which conditions respond best to treatment using herbal medicine. Because the herbalist is based at the Health Centre, it is easy to consult patients' notes and request laboratory tests. The result is a well-integrated approach, where everyone is kept fully informed. There is little doubt that such a set-up is the ideal way in which to practise herbal medicine. Working alongside a full healthcare team allows all members of that team to see how comfortably herbal medicine lies alongside conventional practice. It also allows any misconceptions to be dispelled, and the patients make sure that their doctors are fully aware of how things are progressing from their angle.

Wapping Health Centre is a practice involved in the training of medical students, who routinely spend two weeks clinical experience in general practice. As part of this they are timetabled to spend a day with the medical herbalist, which provides a good opportunity to inform students accurately about a branch of complementary medicine that they are usually unfamiliar with. They do not receive formal training in any branch of complementary medicine, although some medical schools do provide a basic introduction. To date, not surprisingly, the greater majority of them have declared that they thought herbal medicine was 'Chinese', and they did not appreciate how wide a range of applications it has. Perhaps the most useful aspect of their visit is the opportunity they have to talk with the patients, who are the best witnesses to its efficacy; they are only too keen to recount their stories. Interestingly, the over-riding comment from the students is that they are surprised how positive the patients are towards their treatment, and how they seem to take a great interest in it. This is a reflection of the deliberate attempt by the herbalist to ensure that patients realize that they have as important a role as the practitioner in getting well.

Recently, in addition to participating on the local GP training scheme, the herbalist has also been able to accommodate GP registrars who would like to sit in on sessions. Once again, this is an ideal opportunity to let other GPs see just how well herbal medicine fits into a health centre setting. It is hoped that they will not only leave far better informed, but may be inspired to involve herbal medicine in their own future practice. Providing this type of experience for medical students and GP registrars is one of the best ways in which to clearly demonstrate that herbal medicine is effective, and is very popular with the patients.

Be positive

Much has been written regarding patient–practitioner relationships. This is a highly important factor in herbal medicine, since the time a patient spends with a practitioner is comparatively long – the initial consultation of at least one hour is followed up by two-weekly appointments of 30–40 minutes. Thus, a good rapport needs to be established early on. The successful practitioner is one who is able to convey a genuine interest in patients (rather than their medical condition), as well as an enthusiasm for herbal medicine. Sadly, there are all too many practitioners who have lost enthusiasm for their own particular specialities, and this lack of 'sparkle' is very easily picked up by patients. It is also worth remembering that patients may well have consulted a whole series of such people before deciding to book an appointment with the medical herbalist, and a positive informed approach is just what they are seeking.

The effect of adopting a positive approach during a consultation has been considered within orthodox medicine. It formed the basis of a study entitled *General Practice Consultations: Is there any Point in being Positive?* (Thomas, 1987). The research centred on under-diagnosed patients, defined as those for whom no firm diagnosis could be made. They presented with a range of symptoms but no abnormal signs, and were allocated to one of four types of consultation, each group totalling 50 patients. There were 'positive' consultations with or without treatment, and 'negative' consultations with or without treatment. A positive consultation consisted of a diagnosis being given, together with an assurance that the patient would show an improvement in a few days. In the negative consultations, the patient was not offered a diagnosis and no assurance was given. An element of doubt was deliberately introduced by the practitioner, and the patient was told to return in a few days. Those in each category who received 'treatment' received thiamine hydrochloride 3 mg tabs, used as a placebo. No treatment corresponded to no prescription. At the end of each consultation, patients were told that a patient satisfaction survey was being carried out, and they were invited to fill in a questionnaire detailing aspects of doctor–patient communication. Two weeks later, they were sent a card asking about their progress.

Not surprisingly – and most reassuringly – the findings show that there is a point in being positive. After two weeks, 64 per cent of the patients who had received a positive consultation had recovered, compared with 39 per cent of those who had received a negative consultation. Following a survey of patient satisfaction, the patients predictably gave a favourable response to the positive approach and a correspondingly unfavourable response to the negative one. Part of the written questionnaire involved asking whether patients had seen the doctor they wanted to see. It was found that there was a 64 per cent recovery rate for those seeing the doctor for whom they expressed a preference, compared with 45 per cent for those who did not.

However, the study also prompts some interesting questions. When a practitioner introduces an element of doubt regarding a diagnosis, does this have a direct reflection on the rate of recovery? There will always be situations where a firm diagnosis cannot be made, and an honest approach dictates that the patient be made aware of this. The rather authoritarian approach, where the practitioner is all-knowing and always makes a firm diagnosis, is fast disappearing. There is increasing emphasis on better communication between doctor and patient, making the consultation more of a two-way encounter.

In terms of the results of the above study, does this mean that consultations, because they are more honest, are automatically becoming more negative? The answer to this is very complex indeed, since we are dealing with the relationship between two individuals. There will be many more factors than the ability of the doctor to provide a diagnosis or treatment that will, in practice, determine the patient's response. This will include aspects of the doctor's attitude, such as manner and general approach to the consultation. These are obviously very difficult to measure, and indeed one would gain very little by doing so.

The benefits of an on-site herbalist

Undoubtedly, the presence of a medical herbalist in a NHS health centre setting is a positive asset. In a large practice, there will always be a subset of patients who regularly book appointments for an assortment of ill-defined symptoms such as tiredness, anxiety, headaches, loss of appetite, insomnia, lethargy, etc. In the absence of an overt underlying pathology, the situation can persist over a long period, often a number of years. These patients often simply need time, and a listening ear. Thus, by booking a slot with the medical herbalist, they are assured of an appointment of at least one hour. Many authorities may consider this inappropriate use of consultation time. However, it represents a saving of future GP appointment slots, particularly when patients continue to pursue herbal treatment. Once such patients have been assessed, they do not tend to 'go back into the system' because their conditions improve and they are satisfied.

Sometimes patients recognize that they have very minor problems, such as uncertainties regarding diet, and feel guilty about booking an appointment with a doctor. In any case, most GPs cannot deal with detailed questions about diet, which does not constitute a major part of their education. It is, however, central to the training of a medical herbalist. Another type of patient that undoubtedly benefits is the extremely anxious individual. Many people harbour serious worries about their medical conditions, however minor, and by sitting down with a practitioner who has time to listen, they are able to discuss their concerns in a quiet, unhurried manner. They can unburden their worries, and go home far better informed.

At Wapping Health Centre, patients may be referred to the resident medical herbalist by their own GP, although there is also a self-referral system. They are offered this opportunity because it is evident that a consultation could well prevent future health problems. In terms of overall benefit to the Health Centre, certain categories of patient will, if not dealt with, account for a large number of GP consultation slots. In many cases their condition will worsen, requiring yet more treatment, which in the long term increases costs and may involve inappropriate use of drugs such as antidepressants. Where there are many factors combining to give rise to a complicated set of symptoms, it is only reasonable to expect that only an in-depth examination of all the interacting factors will allow the most effective treatment to be selected. Examples of conditions with multifactorial aetiologies include irritable bowel syndrome (IBS), which is discussed in Chapter 9, and chronic fatigue syndrome (CFS). These are conditions that respond very well to herbal medicine because the practitioner has the time to consider all the various aspects. The fact that no two patients with such conditions will present with precisely the same symptoms is perfectly matched by the fact that no two herbal tincture prescriptions are identical. Furthermore, the tincture can be modified at each follow-up if necessary in order to reflect changes in symptoms. This greatly contrasts with the standard treatment for these conditions. As far as the medical herbalist is concerned, there can be no standard treatment for conditions that present in so variable a manner. It is noteworthy that this variability in presentation sets a real problem for researchers in mainstream medicine. Conditions such as IBS attract a great deal of research because they are so frequently encountered in general practice and account for a large number of hospital referrals. The overwhelming majority of research papers conclude that, in considering the effect of, say, a smooth muscle inhibitor or psychotherapy on IBS in a large sample of patients, these treatments had little more than a placebo effect. Naturally some patients will improve, since the particular medication (for example, a smooth muscle relaxant) may relieve muscle spasm in an IBS patient when it is this which is the predominant feature. In others where, for example, the diet is very poor, no amount of such medication will solve the problem, and the situation will not improve until the diet is taken into account and modified accordingly. Likewise, psychotherapy will be of no use unless stress or some other psychological factor is the predominant factor for that particular patient. Once full details of the condition have been elucidated, two other aspects, namely diet and lifestyle, are covered in detail – two aspects usually given little or no consideration by GPs, owing to very severe limitations on consultation times. Since diet is so important to a medical herbalist, this has been considered in a separate chapter.

Lifestyle

In this handbook, only a condensed version of the relevant aspects of this broad topic is possible. The following are the factors that a herbalist will attempt to take into consideration when assessing the patient and deciding on a management plan.

First, it is very difficult to define 'lifestyle'; this concerns aspects of a person's day-to-day living that may have an impact on that person's wellbeing. It encompasses areas such as spiritual beliefs, sports, hobbies, exercise, relationships, nature of employment, housing situation, etc. Detailed statistics on lifestyle can be found in the publication *Social Trends* (HMSO, 1996), which provides information on changing trends in social and cultural activities, from the number of hours weekly spent sleeping to preferred leisure activities. Diet is also a major aspect of lifestyle, and this is why it has been considered separately in detail. It is under this section that alcohol intake and problems with eating disorders can be appreciated. All these factors can contribute to the overall health status and may, individually or collectively, play a role in producing the state generally termed 'stress', which is also hard to define. Stress may, however, be viewed as an unreasonable amount of external pressure that results in recognizable symptoms expressed mainly but not exclusively within the nervous system. Headaches are very common. Excessive worry or nervous strain needs to be assessed by the herbalist, as it undoubtedly has a direct link with several body systems, exacerbating gastrointestinal and skin problems in particular.

The point of prescription

Patients expect prescriptions, and there is considerable pressure for doctors to prescribe during a consultation. Palmer (1992) suggests some reasons for this. Firstly, patients frequently demand prescriptions, although it has been estimated that 20 per cent do not have them dispensed. There is also the pressure of pharmaceutical advertising, and a variety of social factors are involved for the GP. Palmer suggests several of the latter, including playing for time (until normal recovery occurs), keeping face with patients, demonstration of concern, avoidance of confrontation, covering of uncertainty, and hastening the conclusion of the consultation. Finally, there is the 'Friday afternoon antibiotic' syndrome – keeping faith with the other GPs in the practice. Repeat prescriptions are also a problem; they are estimated to account for two-thirds of all items prescribed in general practice (House of Commons and National Audit Office, 1993). This represents 80 per cent of the total cost of prescriptions. Once repeat prescriptions are started, they are difficult to stop; over 25 per cent of the population of the UK is now on regular medication, and this figure increases to 90 per cent in those over 75 years (Harris and Dajda, 1996).

The response to placebos is high; psychologists have even described certain personality traits that identify those most likely to respond, and these include sociability, extroversion and neuroticism. However, the conclusion appears to be that most individuals will respond to placebos, given the right circumstances. Responses are not entirely psychological; some real physiological changes have been recorded, including lowered blood glucose levels and reduced blood pressure. Interestingly, up to 40 per cent of patients may experience side effects following the administration of a placebo, including headache, nausea, diarrhoea and palpitations. Tablet size and colour seem to be important. The most effective are those that are either very small or very large, unlike everyday medicines in appearance, and bitter to the taste.

It is vital that people understand the difference between a prescription for allopathic drugs and that for a herbal preparation. The latter is usually in the form of a tincture, which is of variable composition and can be regularly altered depending on the response obtained. It is normally quite slow to act and must be taken regularly, usually over a period of several weeks. Regular doses ensure that the active constituents are present in the bloodstream and constantly exerting their effects on the tissues at a relatively low level of concentration. Hence the herbalists' reference to the 'promotion of self-healing'. Very rarely are large doses of any one herb administered, as this would not act to support homeostasis in the above way.

Because the herbal prescriptions at Wapping Health Centre are written out on a standard FP10, it is all too easy for the patients to think of them in exactly the same manner as an 'ordinary' drug. They will not act in the same way, and this has to be made clear. Today's society is used to obtaining fast symptomatic relief. To relieve a headache one takes analgesics, and the expectation is that, in a very short time, they will relieve the pain. Herbal medicines do not act in this way, so their action cannot be directly compared with allopathic drugs. Herbal preparations are rarely given to provide symptomatic relief. The approach to treating a simple headache would be to consider in detail the cause of the symptom, which involves as full an investigation as any other seemingly more complex condition.

It is explained to the patients that, in taking a tincture, a 'cocktail' of all the plant constituents is being taken, and the medicine usually contains four or five different species. Thus it is a very complex medicine since, apart from the main active principles, it contains several thousand different substances. An allopathic drug on the other hand is a single substance given at a very much higher concentration than, a naturally occurring substance, present within the plant. Furthermore, although many drugs have been extracted from plants they bear little resemblance to their original forms in that they often occur combined with other molecules; for example sugars, forming glycosides. This means that the aglycone (non-sugar) component will be metabolized in an entirely different manner when hydrolysed and separated from the sugar. This is just one reason why herbalists believe that taking the whole plant tincture provides natural protection from the more potent isolated molecules, since they are more safely metabolized in their naturally occurring forms. It is also the reason why whole plant extracts are generally slow in action.

With regard to repeat prescriptions for herbal medicines, none are allowed without a review consultation. In any case it would be relatively unusual to prescribe more of exactly the same tincture, since its composition is usually altered in response to the change in symptoms. The latter cannot be ascertained without detailed feedback from the patient. In those cases where patients are on long-term medication, for example in the control of the symptoms of rheumatoid arthritis, the patient is reviewed on a monthly basis.

References

Harris, C. M. and Dajda, R. (1996). The scale of repeat prescribing. *Br. J. Gen. Pract.,* **46**, 649–53.

HMSO (1996). *Social Trends 1996.* HMSO.

House of Commons and National Audit Office. Comptroller and Auditor General. (1970). *Repeat Prescribing by General Medical Practitioners in England.* HMSO.

Palmer, K. T. (1992). *Reference Notes for the MRCGP.* Blackwell Science.

Thomas, K. B. (1987). General practice consultations: is there any point in being positive? *Br. Med. J.,* **294**, 1200–1202.

Suggested reading

Zermansky, A. G. (1996). Who controls repeats? *Br. J. Gen. Pract.,* **46**, 643–7.

DIET.

Figure 4.1. *Village doctor*: 'Well, are you better? Have you taken your medicine regularly, and eaten plenty of animal food?'
Patient: 'Yes, sir, I tried it, and so long as it were be-ans and o-ats, I could manage pooty well, sir; but when you come to that there chopped hay, that right-down choked me, sir!'

4

Focus on diet

Food for thought

At Wapping Health Centre successful treatment is often achieved by controlling aspects of the patients' diet, and frequently no tinctures or other medicines are required. This demonstrates that, in contrast to orthodox medicine, the prescription is not necessarily the first line of attack.

A consideration of diet is of the utmost importance. Up to 50 per cent of a patient's treatment by a herbalist is often through modification of diet. It would be fair to say that, even in mainstream allopathic medicine, far better results could be achieved with even a brief look at diet. However, it is obvious that the investigation of diet could take up the whole of the consultation time allocated to a GP, and this is clearly impractical.

At Wapping Health Centre the GPs are at a considerable advantage in being able to refer patients directly to the on-site herbalist, who can therefore give prompt advice as part of the patients' ongoing management without the need for them to travel elsewhere or fund private treatment. Thus, compliance is excellent.

Homework is important

All new patients are given a diet diary to complete before any dietary advice is offered (Fig. 4.2). They are requested to fill it out for a minimum of two weeks, and to bring it with them to their follow-up session. It is of paramount importance to find out precisely what patients are eating before any changes are suggested. Full details of their current diet may provide invaluable information regarding likely causative factors in terms of individual food items. A detailed day-by-day record is essential, and this is the purpose of the diet diary. It has been designed to be small enough for the patient to carry around, but large enough to record all items ingested in a day on a single page. The reverse of each page is headed 'Notes', and

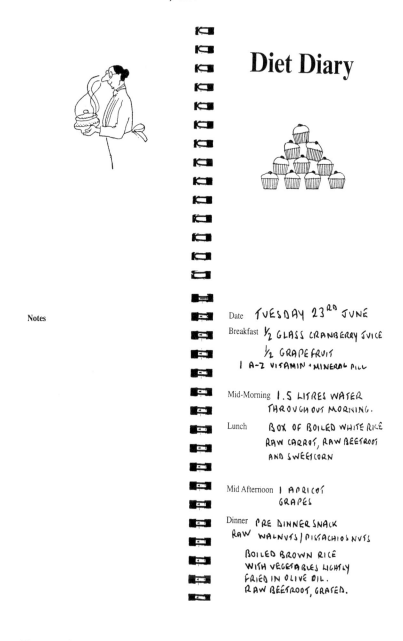

Diet Diary

Notes

Date   TUESDAY 23RD JUNE

Breakfast ½ GLASS CRANBERRY JUICE
  ½ GRAPEFRUIT
  I A-Z VITAMIN + MINERAL PILL

Mid-Morning I.5 LITRES WATER
  THROUGHOUT MORNING.

Lunch   BOX OF BOILED WHITE RICE
  RAW CARROT, RAW BEETROOT
  AND SWEETCORN

Mid Afternoon I APRICOT
  GRAPES

Dinner PRE DINNER SNACK
RAW WALNUTS / PISTACHIOS NUTS

  BOILED BROWN RICE
  WITH VEGETABLES LIGHTLY
  FRIED IN OLIVE OIL.
  RAW BEETROOT, GRATED.

Figure 4.2. Diet diary showing (above) front and back covers and (below) a patient's entry.

patients are asked to make a comment as to how they feel each day, and also to record any changes in symptoms (for example, for patients with eczema this would involve commenting on the state of the skin; in the case of those with IBS, their bowel habit would be recorded, as well as any change in abdominal pain, etc.). In the large majority of cases patients will, without prompting, comment on how certain foods are quite definitely implicated, and note that they hadn't realized exactly what these items were until they started formally recording their diet. It may be imagined that the last thing patients want is to be sent away by their practitioner with homework to do. Our experience indicates quite the opposite, since they all return, diet diaries in hand. Of course it is true to say that the diet diaries are completed in varying degrees of detail. Some patients get carried away and give quantities of foods, or list brand names. Others write a mini essay on their symptoms in the 'notes' section. However, all are remarkably honest, and it is common to find a 'sorry' beside the mention of a chocolate bar! For a good proportion of patients, completing the diary extends well beyond the initial two-week period as they come to realize how useful it is in helping to understand the relevance of diet to their particular condition. There are several patients who are on at least Volume 3 of their diary, and are still going strong. Additional diaries are never denied, since this is considered an important part of the treatment. In some long-term conditions, such as chronic fatigue syndrome (CFS), it will be found that looking over past notes is one of the only ways that a patient can say 'yes, I have made progress' because there is a written record showing that the symptoms have changed with the diet modifications. There is no better proof that diet is important than records kept by patients themselves.

It is thus evident just how important this day-by-day listing of foods is for those conditions where the practitioner is seeking to identify foods that are likely to be aggravating factors; indeed, patients often get there first. In doing so, they have learned for themselves just what they can and cannot eat, and of course they feel fully in control of their treatment. If dietary advice is handed out before patients have been asked to give the current picture, then all such information will be lost. Patients may also become influenced by the practitioner's comments on diet, to the extent that a less than accurate picture is presented – particularly if the patients concerned are aware that their diet is a poor one. It is far better to delay the discussion of diet until the follow-up session, when, armed with the completed diet diary, it can be gone through in detail and modifications introduced. It is unwise to present a lot of detailed information in the initial appointment, when patients are beginning to build up a rapport with their new practitioner. The initial session will have included a lot of questioning about their presenting complaint and past medical history, so it is very useful to be able to send patients away with some homework to do, rather than bombard them with a lot of inevitably detailed questions about their diet.

For the sake of the notes, a basic idea of the patient's typical daily diet is usually requested during the initial consultation, but obviously this is only a very general picture of the kind of food being eaten. For example, it will establish whether the patient is vegetarian or vegan, the average daily intake of tea/coffee, whether the patient is having regular meals, and what general type of diet it is (e.g. lots of 'junk' food). It will also record whether the patient has any food allergies. In herbal medicine, it is very important to record this. Should a patient indicate an allergy to a particular fruit or vegetable, it is a wise precaution to avoid prescribing any herb from the same family in case it precipitates a mild allergic reaction.

Food allergy and intolerance: fact or fiction?

Three main causes of food intolerance have been identified. Firstly there may be a genetic abnormality leading to deficiency of a particular enzyme; for example lack of galactose-1-phosphate uridyl transferase can lead to metabolic disturbance if galactose is ingested. Secondly, intolerance may be due to the presence of a chemical in a food. The well-known 'Chinese restaurant syndrome' is brought about by ingestion of the additive monosodium glutamate. Thirdly, the intolerance may be brought about following the development of an allergic state characterized by hypersensitivity reactions. Although there are four types of the latter, only type I reactions are of direct relevance to the digestive system. Allergic individuals are more likely to form IgE in response to exposure to antigenic allergens, and this tendency is often inherited. Generally speaking, the term 'food allergy' is reserved for the latter reactions; that is, those principally involving the immune system. The remaining reactions are usually referred to as examples of food intolerance.

A disturbing number of patients claim that they have been tested and found to be allergic to a wide variety of foods. The tests they have been subjected to range from hair analysis to skin allergy testing — with a lot of questionable unscientific methods in between. It is now well known that skin testing is totally inappropriate for food intolerance. Often the tests are carried out on the spot in supermarket car parks and other similarly unsuitable environments, without any professional supervision. Since there is no follow-up to such activities, the main motive is profit from what is perceived to be a relatively harmless activity. However, many people follow the suggested diet plans to the letter, and endure unnecessarily restrictive diets, developing serious anxiety. In fact, it is this anxiety that usually prompts them to see the herbalist.

Some of the most unlikely candidates for allergic response have been quoted, including vegetables such as parsnips. Yeast and wheat appear on over 90 per cent of the result sheets. Interestingly, a survey carried out by Guy's Hospital found that the incidence of intolerance to yeast was 3 per cent, and that to wheat 9 per cent (Lessof *et al.*, 1980). A large number of women have placed themselves on a yeast-free diet in the belief that it will help clear Candida, which is a fungal infection. The diagnosis of a Candida infection is in itself a problem. Although it is relatively simple to detect when growing on the oral mucosa or when it is present as vaginal thrush, it is very difficult to prove its existence in the gut. Hence it is easy to attribute a whole array of symptoms, including diarrhoea and bloating, to a Candida outbreak. The link between ingesting yeast (which is also a fungus) and Candida is highly tentative, and a survey amongst patients at Wapping Health Centre revealed that not a single patient was able to explain the reason for omitting yeast-containing items from the diet. Furthermore, despite the explosion of articles on Candida and diet in women's magazines and the promotion of the yeast-free diet, no explanation ever appears. Where a diagnosis has been substantiated, however, the reduction of sugar intake does make biological sense, since fungi thrive on monosaccharide sugars.

The media attention on food allergy has created a whole sub-set of patients who are unnecessarily anxious about their diet. Despite the fact that as many as one in five people in Britain believe they are allergic to one or more foods, studies have found that only about two per cent show any real intolerance (Ameghino, 1998). At Wapping, the experience is that the incidence of true allergy to yeast and wheat is very low (under 10 per cent), and at least 90 per cent of those 'diagnosed' as being allergic are successfully reintroduced to these foods. It is high time that irresponsible testing is prohibited, and it should become the domain of hospital specialists and qualified practitioners only. There is no accurate way of diagnosing food intolerance; the only way to investigate a particular intolerance is via an exclusion diet, which can be a lengthy process. A detailed consideration of this appears in Brostoff and Gamlin (1989).

Time for change

Dietary advice must be realistic. It is pointless to modify a patient's diet to the extent that the patient is left with an unrealistic plan. This is undoubtedly the main reason why much dietary advice is ignored. Any advice offered must be with the individual patient in mind. It must never be a list of general advice that is so general it is useless. Unfortunately this is all too often the case, even when the digestive system is the primary system involved in the condition. At Wapping Health Centre, a lot of patients arrive with the diagnostic label IBS (irritable bowel syndrome). One of the questions that all new patients are asked as part of the diet information sheet is 'Have you ever been recommended a diet by a medical practitioner as part of your treatment?'. One would imagine that, since IBS is a gastrointestinal disorder, the standard approach to treatment might have included some consideration of diet somewhere in the past medical history. However, the commonest answer to the above question is 'No'. The only diet that has been recommended to the small percentage that respond affirmatively (approximately 5 per cent) is a general reference to a 'high fibre diet'. Unfortunately this is one of the worst recommendations that can be offered because, in the absence of any explanation (once again owing to lack of time and/or inclination), the patient will respond by diligently seeking out foods which are promoted as 'high fibre'. Many of these are the worst type of food that an IBS patient can eat. This is discussed further in Chapter 9.

The reasons for reluctance to change are many and varied. It is the herbalist's job to ensure that any changes made are reasonable ones, and that patients view them as such. Indeed, they should always be asked how difficult a particular change is likely to be. It should never be implied that it is 'easy' to make changes in eating habits. It is not, and one only has to consider how we might view being asked to change our own diets to appreciate this. People are highly variable in terms of the willpower required to alter their diet; some patients comment that they would do anything to feel better, whilst others genuinely find it very difficult to implement even the smallest of changes. Thus change in diet, where necessary, needs to become regarded as an important part of the treatment – as important as the prescription.

So how does the medical herbalist tackle the subject of dietary change when a patient hands over the completed diet diary? Firstly, it should be looked at in detail with the patient, then and there. For each day, the 'good' points (such as fresh fruit and vegetables, sufficient fluid intake, etc.) should all be pointed out, leading to an overall positive approach. Where it is necessary to suggest omitting certain items, it is best to write out a short list for future reference. Every suggestion must be explained if it is to be taken on board. It may be necessary to point out that the reason for an item being omitted is not the food itself, but that it contains one particular additive (such as monosodium glutamate). This reasoned, positive approach makes for excellent compliance, and invariably patients will end the session by informing their practitioner that they have learned a lot. They will also become used to enquiring about the content of other foods, and a medical herbalist needs to be fully conversant with the chemical constituents of a range of processed foods.

Finance is frequently quoted as a factor for the inability to change diet, but it is usually an overstated one. A patient on a nutritionally poor diet is often found to be spending relatively large amounts of money on take-away meals or 'junk' food such as beefburgers, as well as on pre-prepared convenience meals. In fact, simple staple dietary items such as pasta, potatoes and rice are not only nutritionally far superior, but are also much cheaper. In such cases, laziness, lack of time or poor education are the true key factors. There are of course instances where patients genuinely experience great difficulty in preparing such items due to lack of suitable cooking facilities – as in the case of some hostels. Likewise, where circumstances dictate that patients eat meals provided by their place of work or where food is included with their accommodation, they have very little control over what their diet comprises. Even so, attempts should still be made to suggest realistic ways of improving on their diet; often all that is required is some very simple advice, such as eating more items that require little or no preparation – fresh fruit and vegetables, or dried fruit.

Many practitioners are of the opinion that such advice is obvious, which is usually far from the case. It should also be remembered that in trying to suggest ways of improving the patients' present situation, however bleak, the practitioner is indicating a genuine concern and interest.

There is much ignorance amongst the general population regarding the components of a healthy well-balanced diet. Although diet and other related topics are endlessly featured in the media, this cannot possibly replace a thorough understanding of what the body cells actually need to function healthily. Knowledge of such aspects, usually only obtained from formal biology or nutrition courses, is not the rule, but it is pleasing to note that teenagers are asked to consider some aspects of diet as part of their GCSE or A-Level biology studies. However, needless to say, for those who do not follow such courses knowledge remains very limited.

At school

School students are a special case; the incidence of conditions such as eczema and asthma is high in this age group and thus school meals are an important factor in their management. Considerable peer pressure underlies the widespread eating of 'fashionable' snacks, which are often highly coloured and/or flavoured – especially crisps, sweets and canned drinks. Although many children are affected by these additives, the temptation to conform is overwhelming, and this is understandable. The role of advertising is very powerful, as demonstrated by a recent experiment with nursery school children in Wales. At the beginning of the school day, the children were shown a short video (*Food Dudes*) where the heroes and their followers ate fresh fruit and vegetables. Following this, the children began to demand the same food and rejected their previous favourites – which included fast food (World in Action, 1998).

The herbalist's role is to present and explain the evidence available regarding how diet may affect asthma, eczema and similar conditions, in a manner appropriate to the child's age. The teenage years are the most difficult to deal with, since this is when peer pressure to conform is the greatest. Ignorance as to why they should avoid certain foods is common. It can never be assumed that an older child with one of these conditions is aware of the link with certain components of the diet. Many a herbalist has omitted to discuss this matter because it was assumed that the parents must have considered diet somewhere along the line. It is a tempting assumption, since those consulting a medical herbalist may well do so as a 'last resort'; however, this certainly does not mean that diet has received attention in previous consultations. Also it needs to be stressed that, although cutting down on a suspect food is a good first step, only leaving it out altogether will allow any valid conclusions to be made regarding whether it really is an aggravating factor. It should be explained that this is due to the cells' extreme sensitivity; they will react to the smallest quantity of the substance in question. If this point is not stressed, a reduction in intake of a particular food could result in very little improvement and the patient incorrectly concluding that it 'makes no difference', when in fact the experiment has only just started. Questioning of patients reveals that they often equate a severe reduction of intake of, for example, milk to giving it up, and they will often comment that they now 'only take it in tea or coffee'. However, this is enough to precipitate a reaction in a hypersensitive individual. Listings of guaranteed milk-free foods are prepared by several large supermarkets; for example, Sainsbury's prepare a whole series of such reference booklets.

Many schools allow the option of bringing packed lunches. This partially solves the problem in that parents have some control over what their child is eating. However, it doesn't remove the peer pressure factor altogether. There are always ways of attempting to overcome this; substituting plain ready-salted crisps for the flavoured versions may provide a 'safer' snack. Also, diet drinks such as colas and lemonades should be discouraged because they simply introduce another unnecessary chemical – an artificial sweetener – into the diet. There is still much controversy regarding the use of such sweetening agents.

The elderly

Those in retirement form another special group with respect to dietary requirements. They are most likely to have been eating a well-established set diet for a large number of years, and changing their eating habits therefore becomes quite a challenge. An analysis of diet diaries completed by patients at Wapping Health Centre confirms that those over 60 years of age purchase fewer processed convenience meals, do more home-cooking and also eat fewer snacks. Thus their intake of artificial additives is low in comparison with the lower age groups, where 'snacking' has become a regular habit.

This possible rigidity in terms of eating habits should always be appreciated by the practitioner. It is pointless trying to establish a new diet for an 80-year-old who is enjoying a less-than-ideal diet; rather, it is more sensible to try a slight modification – for example, the introduction of a wider range of vegetables (thus increasing the natural intake of vitamins and minerals). The latter point is chosen as an example since, with reference to data collected at Wapping Health Centre, those over 60 also tend to eat a narrower range of vegetables and fruit than the younger age groups. This is mainly due to the socio-economic factor that the more exotic items (such as bean sprouts, aubergines, peppers, etc.) are a relatively new introduction, and these patients had a well-established diet before the items became routinely available. Also, the cost may be slightly higher than home- or European-produced material.

Diet in the media

The coverage of diet in the media is extremely haphazard. Most features are concerned with weight loss or with specific topics such as the benefits of 'high fibre' diets. In the case of the latter, most people, when questioned, haven't a clue what fibre is, let alone why they need it, but clever and persistent advertising ensures that they eat the appropriate high fibre breakfast cereal. A recent advertisement makes fun of having to eat five bananas in order to obtain the same amount of fibre as in a single serving of a well-known breakfast cereal; however, the two foods aren't even comparable because the fibre is in a different form in the two items. In fact, the form found in the banana is infinitely preferable to that found in the processed breakfast cereal. But who is going to stop to consider this? Such advertisements rely heavily on public ignorance.

The butter debate

The question 'Should I use butter or margarine?' is one frequently asked of the medical herbalist at this Health Centre. On the one hand patients want to consume a natural product; on the other, they are highly tempted by the well-presented margarine marketing ploys, which assure them that a change to modern margarine is a change to a more healthy future. So what are the facts?

Butter is prepared from milk by churning; this causes the fat globules to coalesce and thus a solid product is formed, leaving behind the liquid buttermilk. The fats and oils in cows' milk are high in triglycerides, which are formed from a complex mixture of short-chain fatty acids including butanoic, stearic and oleic acid. Rather than having a sharp melting point, this complex composition produces a solid that melts over a range of temperatures, and this is characteristic of many animal fats. The short hydrocarbon chains can be pushed past each other quite easily, and butter is therefore quite soft in texture. Longer chain hydrocarbons are not so soft (for example, paraffin waxes).

Margarine was first introduced as a butter substitute in 1869, by the French chemist Mege-Mourie, in response to the butter shortage during the Franco-Prussian war. It originally comprised milk, chopped cow's udder and beef fat. Today's version is synthesized from vegetable oils and petroleum-derived chemicals. Linoleic acid is the main fatty acid in many vegetable oils, and the triglycerides formed from this fatty acid are liquid oils due to the presence of double bonds in the molecule. Since margarine manufacturers want a soft solid as the end product, the oil is subjected to hydrogenation (bubbling of hydrogen through the oil in the presence of a nickel catalyst). The resultant replacement of some of the double bonds by single bonds results in more flexible hydrocarbon chains, which pack together easily, and the oil is converted into a soft fat. The elimination of the double bonds confers another advantage; the product is now far less likely to undergo aerobic decomposition in the presence of air and become rancid. To prevent further rancidity, 2-tert-butyl-4-methoxyphenol (BHA), an antioxidant, is added. This serves to inhibit the reaction with oxygen, which would result in the molecule being cleaved. Interestingly, herbs such as thyme, rosemary and sage contain phenolic compounds related to BHA, which are powerful natural antioxidants.

The next stage of margarine manufacture involves the removal of highly pungent by-products by passing steam over the fat, although this also removes the colour. Thus, carotenes are added to restore a butter-like appearance. The buttery odour is created by the addition of butanedione. The nutritional value is enhanced by the addition of vitamins A and D, and the flavour is improved by the emulsification of the fats with skimmed milk containing a culture of Lactobacillus, which produces lactic acid. Lecithins are added to provide overall stability to the product. As can be seen, margarine is a highly processed product, being the result of a complex sequence of reactions. This is in stark contrast to the simple production of butter. Patients are therefore advised that butter, in moderation, is a healthier option than margarine.

To make articles on popular topics appeal to the general public, information can be presented in a manner that may be rather misleading. A newspaper editorial headed 'Ketchup, good for the heart' (Mihill, 1997) is typical of how certain dietary facts are presented. It begins 'Get out the ketchup bottle and live longer, scientists suggested yesterday ...'. The article concerned new research into antioxidants, carried out by the European Union Euramic study group. The highest levels of lycopenes (a chemical group particularly effective in protecting against heart attacks) were found to be present in tomatoes. They concluded that 'in the average [poor] diet, the chief source was tomato ketchup, and tomato sauce found on pizzas'. It is only much further into the article that other more natural sources are listed; watermelon, red grapefruit and shellfish. Including more tomato ketchup in the diet will probably only serve to promote the eating of those items that it normally accompanies, such as chips and 'junk' food, which are items high in lipids. This is ironic in that lycopene is thought to exert its effect on low-density lipoprotein; it is also in direct opposition to the research group's main aim, namely to promote better health.

Fat fads

The obsession with fat-free foods is reaching a peak in America. In many states, obtaining whole-milk dairy products such as yoghurts is virtually impossible. This provides yet another example of the ill-informed attempting to force their dietary fads upon young children. So ridiculous is the situation with items that are deliberately aimed at children that, in an attempt to restore the calorific value of such low-fat items to a level that will meet the children's growth requirements, yoghurts are artificially sweetened to a level of 70 calories by the addition of sugar. Therefore, having responded to the demand for fat-free or low-fat products, the manufacturer has to adjust the composition to provide sufficient calories, and the product ends up with almost as many calories as the healthier, more natural full-fat version. But fat is the enemy, or so it is believed. Accordingly, it is commercially acceptable to substitute fat-derived calories with chocolate drops and 'hundreds and thousands', both of which are common components of children's yoghurts in America. As one observer pointed out, this anti-fat fad is not based on any sound knowledge of nutrition. A large percentage of those parents who feed their family low-fat items visit fast food outlets several times a week (presumably for a fat top-up!).

In Britain, a new margarine is shortly to be available at a cost of six times the price of other margarines. It claims to reduce blood cholesterol levels and has proved very popular in Finland, where it originated. Produced from by-products of the wood pulp industry, it acts by inhibiting cholesterol absorption from the gut, and daily consumption of a minimum of 25 g will reduce the cholesterol level by about 10 per cent. The British Heart Foundation quite correctly points out that, although it is an interesting product, to achieve any significant cholesterol reduction one would have to take in more than the current average daily consumption of margarine. They comment that it would 'increase the total fat intake and might lead down the road to obesity' (Laurence, 1998).

A recent study (February, 1998) by the Centre for Human Nutrition at the University of Sheffield revealed a marked mood change in a group of individuals placed on a low-fat diet. They were offered a large choice of foods, and were given low-fat versions of 'ordinary' items rather than a change in diet. Both depression and aggression increased markedly in the experimental group as compared with the control. This study would appear to have interesting implications, particularly with regard to children placed on an artificially low-fat diet.

Having exhausted all possible variations on the theme of low-calorie products, the dietary foods market is now developing more sophisticated products. One example of these is 'Olibra' yoghurt, which stimulates the small intestine to release peptides that act on the brain to induce satiation. Several nutrition agencies, including the British Nutritional Foundation, are concerned about long-term effects, especially since this yoghurt is only one of a whole range of foods (including drinks, soups, biscuits, etc.) to be released (Durman and Whitworth, 1998).

Ignorance about dietary matters is by no means a minor point to the medical herbalist, who looks at diet in great detail. Establishing a therapeutic background of a good, balanced diet, with adequate supplies of protein, lipid, carbohydrate, mineral salts, vitamins, fibre and water, is essential if treatment is to be optimized. Teaching the patient how to do this is even more important. Well-informed patients will be able to assess for themselves what comprises a sensible diet.

Designer foods?

Encouraging healthy eating is a multi-million pound business, and it has led to the development of a whole new category of products known as 'functional foods'. The latter have been defined as 'foods which have a positive impact on the individual's health, physical performance or state of mind, in addition to their nutritive value' (Goldberg, 1994). However, this is surely close to the definition of food anyway? The lack of food would certainly lead to a negative impact on all those features mentioned in the definition. Perhaps it is yet another case of clever marketing making the public think that these foods are special in some way and, most important of all, that they are vital if one is to remain healthy.

The concept of 'health foods' is an ancient one. In recent years, these items were thought of as being more 'natural' than the 'normal' food on sale and, consequently, only available from a health food shop. They were generally free of additives and were packaged very simply, endorsing the environmentally friendly aspect. In contrast, the new generation of 'functional foods' has a long list of additives, which might range from trace elements to extra amino acids. Whatever they might do, they do not provide these substances in their natural forms and, consequently, it is unlikely that they will be absorbed efficiently by the body. Virtually any substance that has been associated with nutritional studies is a candidate for inclusion in one of these foods. There are pastilles with added antioxidants, and even drinks with added fibre, which seems to defy logic. For those who are keen to improve their 'sports performance', there are specially formulated breakfast cereals, and a whole range of 'sports drinks'. The latter account for approximately 1.5 per cent of the total soft drinks market, and the individual drinks cost an average of £1.50 each, which is several times the cost of the average canned soft drink. A recent study by the Food Commission (*Food Magazine*, October 1997) revealed that almost all were high in sugar, yet only 5 out of the sample of 22 gave a sugar content figure. Many listed only the total carbohydrate content, which, although technically and legally correct, is very misleading. Carbohydrates form a large group of substances, including the monosaccharide sugars such as glucose and the disaccharide examples such as sucrose, as well as the larger molecules such as starch and cellulose. One product was advertised as supplying 'more carbohydrate than two and a half cans of spaghetti, without the bulk'. This gives the false impression that it contains the starches found in pasta, which of course it does not. Two drinks listed in the report contained 18 per cent sugar, with the lowest sugar content being 10 percent. Some of these figures were higher than in the drinks to which they purport to be offering a healthier alternative. Also of relevance is the caffeine level of these designer drinks. Levels recorded in the study were up to three times higher than those typically associated with ordinary cola drinks. Highly dubious claims regarding other ingredients were also questioned; for example, the maker of one drink claimed that the inclusion of the amino acid taurine provides an 'energy transmitter', which, as the commission points out, is meaningless. These pseudo-scientific claims can, yet again, be seen to rely on public ignorance. The Sports Commission concludes: 'For extra energy, a banana is healthier'. This says it all.

The functional foods business is a rapidly growing one; in 1994 it was worth seven billion US dollars, and it is predicted to more than double by the year 2000. With all this ready-formulated food, the general population is encouraged not to think too deeply about diet – it has all been taken care of by the firms producing these items. No wonder people are unable to name foods that are sources of common vitamins and minerals in their diet; these are simply added to most processed foods. The trouble is, adding vitamins and minerals to a basically unhealthy food doesn't improve the overall nutritional value of that food, which may still be a highly coloured and highly flavoured cocktail of chemicals. Ignorance about diet is well catered for – for example, vegetarians can rely on a whole range of ready-prepared meals labelled 'suitable for vegetarians'. It will not be long before fresh fruit and vegetables bear the same label.

Why additives?

Food is essential for any organism. After digestion and absorption, the chemical components of food are taken up by the cells and used in a wide variety of metabolic processes that are essential for sustaining life. Of concern to many people are those chemical substances that do not originate from the food itself, but are present as a result of processing, packaging and storage, etc. These artificial additives receive constant media attention as more and more research revealing their probable harmful effects on the body is published.

There are two main groups of additives: the intentional (included in order to perform a specific function) and the incidental (accidentally incorporated during processing). The total number of recorded incidental additives is over 10 000 different substances, with another 3000 intentional additives. Sugar and salt are at the top of the list and, together with baking powder, citric acid, mustard, pepper, and vegetable-derived dyes, they make up over 98 per cent by weight of all intentional additives. Processing of food unavoidably involves the denaturing of many of its constituents, including certain vitamins, owing to the high temperatures associated with processes like canning. It is therefore common to find vitamins artificially introduced to make up for this deficit. Other chemicals are added to enhance colour and flavour, slow down decomposition, add texture, to bleach, ripen (or prevent ripening) and control moisture content, etc.

Additives: a herbalist's viewpoint

Owing to the media exposure, many patients will express concern about particular additives, and the herbalist needs to respond realistically. In attempting to assess additives in general, their chemical nature and their possible effect on the human body needs to be considered. Some substances classed as additives have been used throughout history (e.g. salt). Others, such as the artificial sweeteners and colours, are a more modern generation of organic molecules, and their effects on the body are not fully known. No matter what current research might be presented, it will not be until they have been around for a long enough period to study their long-term effects that we can accurately assess just how 'harmless' they are. Artificial sweeteners are discussed in a separate section below, since they are becoming a very important factor in dietary advice.

The increasing use of chemical additives is undoubtedly linked to the general public's demand for convenience foods. In choosing a ready-made meal with a relatively long shelf-life, one can expect a correspondingly long list of additives. Most of the population will probably remain unaffected by eating these substances; however, they should be avoided by those who suffer from conditions that are likely to be aggravated by such chemicals. Once again, education is the answer.

Regular 'scare stories' regarding the toxic effects of some of the additives do little to help, although they do act as regular reminders to eat as healthily as possible. The herbalist will also find that patients frequently express their concern about 'chemicals' in their food. The best general rule is a very simple one; eat as much food as possible in the form closest to its natural state. This does not mean eating everything without any cooking (although raw foods are important) but, for example, purchasing raw vegetables and cooking them rather than buying the pre-cooked version. When something is pre-cooked, it must have had a substance added to it to stop it decomposing. With prior thought, this is just one more chemical that can be easily avoided.

How sweet

Nowadays natural sugar is freely available, so why do we need inferior artificial replacements? Apart from those cases where obesity is a serious medical problem, or where metabolic conditions like diabetes mean that sugar intake must be restricted, artificial sweeteners serve no real purpose for the consumer. It is, of course, the link with weight loss that is the main reason for the continued successful marketing of artificial sweeteners; dieting is big business. It would be all very well if these artificial sweeteners were indeed restricted to diet products, but the trend is to 'secrete' small amounts of these products (which are apparently much cheaper than real sugar) into all kinds of foods, including items such as baked beans and pickled onions — and this is always under the guise of being 'more healthy' because there is no sugar. It is unfortunate that most non-diet drinks now contain an artificial sweetener in addition to the sugar content, which means that the consumer is not even allowed the option of a drink that just contains sugar. Incredibly, saccharin is routinely added to tonic water, and there are just two companies in Britain that produce non-diet tonic water without saccharin. This seems especially ironic in that tonic water should be a bitter drink (a feature obtained by the addition of quinine, derived from the bark of the cinchona tree). One of the largest manufacturers of soft drinks removes the saccharin from its tonic water for the overseas market whilst, in the UK, we are given no option. A survey amongst the patients at Wapping Health Centre reveals that, not surprisingly, they only expect to find artificial sweeteners in diet drinks. Very few check the labels of such products, so they continue to assume that non-diet versions only contain sugar. Having been introduced to diet drinks early in life, children develop a taste for them and continue drinking them throughout adult life. The difference in taste between the diet and sugar-based versions of, for example, cola is so marked that the individual concerned finds it very difficult to make a change. We are now observing a whole generation of children brought up in households where purchase of diet drinks is the norm. Could this be a significant factor in the increased incidence of IBS and some allergic conditions?

Saccharin is one of the most frequently utilized substances, and it is most commonly present as the salt sodium saccharin. Approximately 25 per cent of the population describe it as having a bitter, metallic aftertaste, so various additives have to be added to overcome this — the most common being natural sugar. It was accidentally synthesized by the American chemist Constantine Fahlberg. Saccharin and its sodium and calcium salts were first listed as artificial sweeteners in 1959 (Miller and Frattali, 1991).

Artificial sweeteners have not had an easy ride; in the case of saccharin, many studies have demonstrated a link between high levels of dietary intake and bladder cancer (National Academy of Sciences, 1985). In fact, there were so many studies in the USA concluding that it was harmful, the FDA proposed banning it in 1977. This proposed action was based on the Delaney Anti-Cancer Clause, which states that a carcinogenic food additive cannot be found safe under the 1958 Food Additives Amendment to the 1938 Federal Food, Drug and Cosmetics Act. However, special congressional legislation finally allowed its continued use when the Saccharin Study and Labelling Act was passed in 1977. Even so, products containing saccharin had to be accompanied by labels warning of its potential hazard to health:

> Use of this product may be hazardous to your health. This product contains saccharin, which has been determined to cause cancer in laboratory animals.

Supermarkets in the USA prominently display a similar warning on their premises.

Studies carried out by a review panel in 1983 concluded that the physiological changes observed in rats do not occur in humans under 'normal' levels of usage. An extensive study carried out by the

International Research Development Corporation (IRDC) found that the lowest incidence of tumours in rats was at a saccharin level equivalent to 3 per cent of their total diet. Mitchell *et al.* (1991) concluded that this bladder cancer formation is species-specific.

The EU has proposed a directive that specifies the maximum levels of saccharin in various categories of foods; for example, 80 mg/l in non-alcoholic drinks, 100 mg/kg for desserts and 200–1200 mg/kg for confectionary items. Britain expresses relatively little concern regarding saccharin, and there are no health warnings on food labels. In fact, its permitted use is expanding to products such as toothpaste, where it is said to improve palatability. Incredibly, it is also found in some brands of 'natural' spring water, together with a 'hint of fruit'. If real fruit were being added, it would come with the natural sugar produced as a result of photosynthesis.

Another low-calorie sweetener that is commonly included in soft drinks is the dipeptide aspartame. It has a major disadvantage in that it becomes hydrolysed (and consequently loses its sweetness) when subjected to prolonged exposure to water or excessive heat. This, together with its relatively high cost (compared with saccharin), means that it cannot be used in convenience meals. However, it is used in ultra-high temperature (UHT) treatments, when it is added aseptically after the actual heat treatment stage. In the gut, aspartame is rapidly hydrolysed to its constituent amino acids L-phenylalanine and L-aspartic acid, as well as some methanol. It is not absorbed as the intact molecule. Those heterozygous for phenylketonuria (PKU), which is a genetic condition where there is a deficiency in the ability to metabolize phenylalanine, do not have any problems in metabolizing the relatively small amounts of this amino acid found in aspartame. The phenylalanine content in aspartame is in fact less than in meat, dairy products and other protein-containing foods. However, foods containing it must be labelled in order to alert those with this condition because of their need to limit total intake. The proposed EU directive mentioned above proposes a maximum level of 600 mg/l in soft drinks, 1000 mg/kg for desserts and 1000–5000 mg/kg for confectionary items.

In hospital ... and malnourished?

The provision of suitable diets for patients in hospital would seem to be central to their treatment; however, there have been many studies investigating the common phenomenon of hospital under-nutrition. These studies range from those that look at the role of diet in the recovery of patients following specific types of surgical intervention to those that present a general investigation of diet.

Powell-Tuck (1997) concluded that between 20 and 50 per cent of hospital patients are undernourished. This has all kinds of implications, not least financial ones. An undernourished patient has a longer recovery period, and thus an extended hospital stay. For this reason alone, it is surprising that dietary provision has not been more fully investigated by dieticians. Delmi *et al.* (1990) were able to demonstrate a reduction in average length of stay of 16 days in an orthopaedic ward where simple nutritional supplementation was provided. The low priority given to nutrition within the hospital environment is a good indicator of the attitude to diet in general. This is yet another area where its true importance will most probably only emerge as a result of future audits, when attention to patients' diets is seen to save enough money to warrant a serious rethink about the food they are given. This apparent lack of attention to diet within the hospital environment could be taken as a general indication of the perceived importance of diet within some areas of orthodox medicine. A minority of specialists would mention it as a factor in the treatment of their patients and, as previously mentioned, when they do, the advice is so generalized as to be unhelpful. Diet is a highly neglected factor. It is well recognized that under-nutrition affects mood, cognitive function, efficiency of absorption in the gastrointestinal tract, immune function, respiratory and cardiac function, and quality of life. It is now universally accepted that diet is of paramount importance in the treatment of patients with HIV and AIDS.

Case history

An 8-year-old girl presented with a history of chronic diarrhoea and abdominal pain over the last 3 years. This was severe enough to seriously interfere with her schooling. She had been fully investigated by a gastroenterologist, and no serious pathology identified. She then attended Wapping Health Centre and, when questioned about diet, her mother was uncertain as to whether any particular food was precipitating the diarrhoea, which occurred several times a day. No advice regarding diet had been offered by the hospital. Following the taking of a full medical history, the mother was asked to fill in a diet diary for two full weeks, which would be studied in the follow-up appointment.

Detailed analysis of the diet diary revealed a daily breakfast of a bacon sandwich, and regular intake of pork sausages (two to three times per week). Since pork is frequently implicated in diarrhoea and other symptoms indicating gut sensitivity, it was recommended that, as a first step, the bacon and sausages should be omitted. A vegetarian replacement for the sausages was suggested. She was prescribed a low dose of *Ulmus fulva* (slippery elm) tablets (200 mg o.d.).

At the follow-up session, the diarrhoea and abdominal pain had subsided and the girl was enjoying a vegetarian sausage sandwich for breakfast. The mother went on to report one relapse following a visit to a friend's birthday party, where the child had eaten some sausage rolls and some non-dairy ice cream (high in pork fat). This experience confirmed the causative agent, and the value of diet investigation.

References

Ameghino, J. (1998). Is your food allergy a fiction? *The Guardian*, 8 December.

Brostoff, J. and Gamlin, L. (1989). *Food Allergy and Intolerance*. Bloomsbury Publishing Ltd.

Delmi, M., Rapin, C. H., Bengoa J. M. *et al.* (1990). Dietary supplementation in elderly patients with fractured neck of the femur. *Lancet*, **335**, 1013–16.

Durman, P. and Whitworth, D. (1998). 'Smart' yoghurt tricks dieters into feeling full. *The Times*, 9 January.

Goldberg, I. (1994). *Functional Foods*. Chapman and Hall.

Laurance, J. (1998). New spread reduces fat in the body. *The Independent*, 8 October.

Lessof, M. H., Wraith, D. G., Merritt, J. and Buisseret, P. D. (1980). Food allergy and intolerance in 100 patients – local and systemic effects. *Q. J. Med.*, **49**, 259–71.

Mihill, C. (1997). Ketchup 'good for the heart'. *The Guardian*, 16 October.

Miller, S. A. and Frattali, V. P. (1991). In *Sugars and Sweeteners* (N. Kretchmer and C. B. Hollenbeck, eds), pp. 245–55. CRC Press.

Mitchell, M. L., Pearson, R. L. and Saccharin, R. L. (1991). In *Alternative Sweeteners* (L. D. Nabors and R. C. Gelardi, eds), 2nd edn. Marcel Dekker.

National Academy of Science, National Research Council, Committee on the Evaluation of Cyclamate for Carcinogenicity (1985). *Evaluation of Cyclamate for Carcinogenicity*. National Academic Press.

Powell-Tuck, J. (1997). Penalties of hospital under-nutrition. *J. R. Soc. Med.*, **90**, 8–11.

World in Action (1998). *Food Dudes* programme, ITV, 26 November.

Suggested reading

Arnold, D. L., Moodie, C. A., Grice, H. C. *et al.* (1980). Long-term toxicity of ortho-toluenesulfonamide and sodium saccharin in the rat. *Toxic. Appl. Pharmacol.*, **52**, 113–52.

Butchko, H. H. and Kotsonis, F. N. (1989). Aspartame: review of recent research. *Comments Toxicol.*, **3**, 253–78.

Hawkes, N. (1997). The 'sporting' drink with 19 spoons of sugar. *The Times*, 21 October.

Marie, S. and Piggott, J. R. (1991). *Handbook of Sweeteners*. Blackie.

McWhirter, J. and Pennington, C. (1994). Incidence and recognition of malnutrition in hospital. *Br. Med. J.*, **308**, 945–8.

Royal College of Physicians and British Nutrition Foundation (1984). Food intolerance and aversion. *J. R. Coll. Phys.*, **18**, 1–14.

Schiffman, S. S. and Gatlin, C. A. (1993). Sweeteners: state of knowledge review. *Neurosci. Biobehav. Rev.*, **17**, 313–45.

Wells, A. G. (1989). The use of intense sweeteners in soft drinks. In *Progress in Sweeteners* (T. H. Grenby, ed.), pp. 169–214. Elsevier Applied Science.

5
Materials and methods

Formulation of a prescription

At the end of a consultation, a prescription consisting of a mixture of several tinctures may be written out. Generally speaking, a typical formulation would comprise between four and six herbs, the total volume being 100 ml. Sometimes a single herb is prescribed, for example, *Vitex agnus-castus* (chasteberry). There is obviously considerable variation amongst herbalists as to the number of different herbs used. This variation once again reflects the individual approach that is a key feature of herbal medicine. There are quite definitely no 'set formulas' for individual conditions, each prescription being made up individually for each patient (Fig. 5.1).

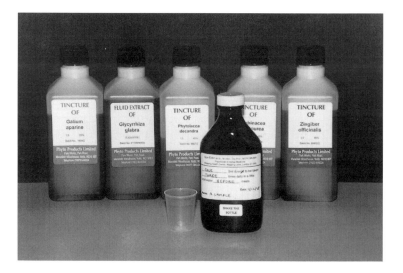

Figure 5.1. The components of a prescription and the dispensed medicine.

At Wapping Health Centre, prescriptions are written out on a standard FP10. A sample prescription is presented in the Appendix.

Table 5.1 Examples of botanical parts used in tinctures.

Part of plant	Example of species used
Flower	*Matricaria recutita* (German chamomile)
Fruits	*Crataegus oxyacantha* (hawthorn)
Seeds	*Apium graveolens* (celery)
Leaves/stems	*Urtica dioica* (nettle)
Roots	*Valeriana officinalis* (valerian)
Bark	*Viburnum opulus* (cramp bark)
Rhizome	*Agropyron repens* (couch grass)

Scientific name

It is essential to give the **full** scientific name, i.e. both genus and species, when listing the herbs. If only the genus is provided there could be great confusion at the point of dispensing, as there are several examples where two or more species from the genus are available. These do not necessarily have a similar action, and cannot therefore be substituted for each other. Examples include *Viburnum opulus* (cramp bark) and *Viburnum prunifolium* (black haw), and *Berberis vulgaris* (bayberry) and *Berberis aquifolium* (oregon grape). Common names are never used; this would be a very dangerous practice, since only the scientific names are universal. Each country, and indeed locality, has a different common name for a given species.

Part of plant

As already stated, a variety of different botanical parts are used to prepare tinctures (Table 5.1). The reference to the particular part of the plant is only given on the actual prescription when several different tinctures are available for one species, each derived from a different part of that plant. For example, tinctures are made from either the root or the shoot system of *Taraxacum officinale* (dandelion). The two tinctures have different actions, so it is vital to indicate which is required. The leaf (denoted HERBA) acts as a diuretic, whereas the root (denoted RADIX) is a cholagogue.

Tincture or fluid extract?

Most prescriptions comprise tinctures that have been prepared as described later in this chapter. In some cases it is necessary to add a more concentrated form of a particular herb, and 'FE' (denoting fluid extract) is then written after the scientific name. Fluid extracts are prepared using equal volumes of fresh plant material and alcohol. Their incorporation into a prescription is very useful where it is important to prescribe a particular herb, but where a normal tincture strength (i.e. 1:3 to 1:10) would mean too great a volume for it to be part of the 100 ml total — which would, of course, decrease the effective concentration of the other herbs. Where a tincture is particularly bitter and it is desirable to improve the taste, a small volume of *Glycyrrhiza glabra* (liquorice) FE is extremely effective — as long as this herb is not contraindicated for the particular condition being treated. This is worth remembering when prescribing for children.

Volumes

Each tincture is expressed as a portion of a total volume of 100 ml. Using this set volume allows all herbal prescriptions to be presented in a standard form. The smallest volume of tincture dispensed is 5 ml per 100 ml total, and such a small volume is reserved for those herbs that are toxic in larger amounts — for example, *Gelsemium sempervirens* (yellow jasmine) — or for those that, although not toxic at higher levels, have an extremely unpleasant taste. For example, *Zingiber officinalis* (ginger) tinctures are very strong (usually 1:2 or 1:3) and extremely 'hot', so not more than 5 ml ginger per 100 ml is prescribed.

Although the remedy is always presented as a total volume of 100 ml on the FP10, the patient may be provided with larger volumes (multiples of 100 ml). This obviously depends on the daily dose and the length of the course of treatment.

Dose

The usual dose for herbal tinctures is 5 ml three times a day; thus, in a week, $7 \times 15 = 105$ ml will be required. Therefore, a 100 ml bottle will last about one week. Since patients are usually reviewed every two weeks, 200 ml is the most commonly prescribed volume. All patients at Wapping Health Centre are provided with 30 ml graduated medicine tumblers, in order that the 5 ml dose can be standardized. Left to their own devices, patients would measure out the 5 ml dose printed on the pharmacist's label using a variety of means, resulting in a huge variation in actual doses (and with a volume of 5 ml this could result in a large error). Results would not then be comparable between patients, and any research data would be unreliable. Also, pouring the 5 ml dose into a 30 ml container means that a maximum of only 25 ml water can be added, and in our experience this is a very useful way of preventing the patient diluting the tincture too much – which only prolongs the awful taste!

The preparation of herbal medicines

In pharmacy, medicines prepared from crude plant material are known as galenicals, and are distinct from isolated substances. As the name suggests, they are named after the Greek physician Galen, who was one of the first people to prepare medicines from plants. They may take several forms; for example tinctures, infusions, tablets, creams and ointments. The official galenical preparations are described in the *British Pharmacopoeia*, and are made from plants of prescribed quality, using standardized pharmaceutical methods. At the beginning of the twentieth century, more than 90 per cent of the medicines listed in the *British Pharmacopoeia* were directly derived from plants. Nowadays, the total for all items derived from plants, including drugs (i.e. isolated substances) of plant origin, is less than 25 per cent. The steady decline in plant-based medicines came as they were replaced by cheaper, synthetic alternatives, although the decline has now levelled out world wide as it is being recognized that it is worthwhile reinvestigating the use of many plant remedies.

Herbal medicines are commonly prescribed in the form of liquids. Once there was a whole range of tinctures, decoctions, fluid extracts, infusions, syrups, vinegars and elixirs, etc. Nowadays, the most commonly prescribed herbal medicine is the tincture.

Tinctures

As stated above, a tincture is the type of medicine routinely prescribed by western medical herbalists. It is a liquid medicine formed by steeping a herb in a solvent in order to extract the chemical constituents, and the aim of the procedure is to achieve maximum extraction. In modern herbal practice the solvent used is ethyl alcohol, either alone or mixed with water. The molecule of ethyl alcohol has both polar and non-polar regions, and so it acts as an ideal solvent for the wide variety of compounds found in plant material. In addition, the alcohol content protects against bacterial decomposition, so the tincture keeps longer than a simple aqueous solution such as an infusion. All tinctures are prepared from unprocessed plant material, and the highest quality ones use fresh plant material immediately following harvest. However, in the case of the preparation of tinctures of tropical species, dried material often has to be utilized. The precise ratio of plant material to ethyl alcohol, and the concentration of alcohol used, varies according to the species. These ratios are all listed in the *British Herbal Pharmacopoeia*. The great majority are formed using one part of fresh plant material to five parts of alcohol.

The variation in the concentration of alcohol allows the best extraction of active principles; where a particular species is rich in those substances that are readily soluble in water, a low alcohol concentration is used. Resins are soluble in alcohol, but insoluble in water. Glycosides are soluble in both solvents. The presence of alcohol is important to control the hydrolysis of glycosides and saponins, and to dissolve important medicinal groups such as alkaloids, resins and essential oils. It also reduces the solubility of some constituents, such as inert gums, that would be undesirable in the final preparation. Alcohol can also inactivate enzymes that may otherwise be responsible for the breakdown of alkaloids. It is vital that heat is not applied during any part of the extraction, as high temperatures may denature any important enzymes present, cause volatile substances such as essential oils to be lost, and increase the solubility of inert substances. As far as the original definition is concerned, a true tincture should not have less than 45 per cent alcohol. This originally allowed a distinction between tinctures and the other two main types of liquid preparations, namely decoctions and infusions.

Depending on the nature of the plant material, it is left in the alcohol for 2–3 weeks. If it is relatively soft, as in the case of leaves, then two weeks will suffice. If there is a considerable amount of woody material, as when dealing with bark, older stems or roots, then the extraction will take a little longer. The result is a potent, brownish, alcoholic liquid. The important point to note is that no further modification is made, although in some cases (where there are a lot of suspended solids) it may be filtered. This is the medicine that is prescribed; it is not diluted or processed in any way.

Fluid extracts are concentrated extracts of plant material in either alcohol or water. The ratio of plant material to solvent should be 1:1. These are therefore the most concentrated forms of liquid medication available.

The following account relates to the preparation of a tincture of *Urtica dioica* (nettle) as carried out by Granary Herbs of Bearsted (see Appendix), who specialize in the production of tinctures from organically grown plants. Several other companies produce tinctures on a larger scale.

The nettles are harvested during the summer, and immediately macerated. 700 g are weighed out and placed in a clear glass jar. The foliage is pressed down well in the container and 525 ml of 96 per cent ethyl alcohol is added. To this is added 1575 ml water. The lid is then placed in position and the jar shaken well, and the material is left for 3 weeks so that the extraction of the chemical constituents of the plant material can take place. The container is shaken at regular intervals. After this period of time, the fluid is poured off and the solid plant material is put in a winepress to extract the remaining fluid. This is added to that which was decanted off, and the tincture removed to a stock bottle. No modifications are made to the resultant tincture, which has been obtained in as natural a way as possible. It is then dispensed into bottles, which are dispatched to the herbalist's dispensary. Because of the alcohol content, the tinctures can be stored at room temperature without any fear of decomposition. Once the initial extraction process is over it is preferable to keep the alcoholic tincture in dark glass bottles, since some species contain substances that decompose on exposure to sunlight.

Details of all the tinctures used in western herbal medicine can be found in the *British Herbal Pharmacopoeia*. This lists monographs detailing botanical descriptions (microscopic and macroscopic), actions, indications and dosages (Fig. 5.3).

Chemical constituents

Although the following notes deal with some biochemical aspects of individual components, the fact remains that the medicinal effect of most components was first noted after administration of whole plant extracts.

Saponins

These compounds are well known for producing 'foam' in aqueous solution, and they are the main constituents of *Saponaria officinalis* (soapwort). Historically, the roots of this plant have been used as a soap substitute. Saponins occur naturally as glycosides – that is, in combination with either a sugar molecule or the closely related glucuronic acid. If present intact in the bloodstream, saponins would cause haemolysis of the erythrocytes; it is this property that has given them a somewhat negative image. This is undeserved since, when taken by mouth, the saponin is hydrolysed to its constituents – a sugar and an aglycone (sapogenin) – and neither of these products cause haemolytic activity. This difference in toxicity between the isolated and combined forms is yet another illustration of how important detailed knowledge of biochemistry is; injection of

LAPPA ROOT

SYNONYMS
Burdock Root; Bardane Root.

DEFINITION
Lappa Root consists of the dried underground parts of *Arctium lappa* L. (Fam. Compositae) gathered during the first year of growth. The plants are native British herbs, biennial, with long petioled, somewhat woolly, cordate ovate leaves up to 40 cm long, forming a rosette in the first year.
Lappa Root contains a bitter principle and much inulin.
Martindale, 25th Edn., p. 1531. B.P.C. (1934), p. 586.

DESCRIPTION OF CUT ROOT
Macroscopical: Split, cylindrical pieces of root, the outer surface covered with brown cork and very longitudinally wrinkled, the inner surface mealy, buff-white. Taste mucilaginous and slightly bitter.

Microscopical: Xylem of lignified vessels up to 100 μm in diameter, reticulately thickened or with bordered pits. Sclerenchyma of a few, thin-walled lignified fibres. Mainly parenchyma, with many angular, pseudo-crystalline slightly birefringent masses of inulin giving no response to iodine water, and with a few grains of starch.
U.S.D., 22nd Edn., p 593.

Total Ash: Not more than 10%.

Acid Insoluble Ash: Not more than 3%.

Foreign Organic Matter: Not more than 2%.

THERAPEUTICS
Action: Diuretic. Orexigenic.

Indications: Cutaneous eruptions. Rheumatism. Cystitis. Gout. Anorexia nervosa.

Specific Indications: Eczema, especially in dry and desquamatory phase. Psoriasis.

Combinations used: Combines well with Rumex Crispus or Trifolium Pratense in skin disease.

Preparations and Dosage: (thrice daily)
Dried root 2-6 g or by infusion. Liquid Extract 1:1 in 25% alcohol. Dose 2-8 ml. Tincture 1:10 in 45% alcohol. Dose 8-12 ml. Decoction 1:20. Dose 500 ml/day.

Figure 5.3. Extract from the *British Herbal Pharmacopoeia*, by permission of the British Herbal Medicine Association.

LAVANDULA

SYNONYMS

Lavender; Lavender Flowers; Lavendula spica L.

DEFINITION

Lavandula consists of the flowers of *Lavandula officinalis* Chaix. (Fam. Labiatae), an evergreen shrub 1 metre in height, indigenous to Southern Europe but extensively cultivated in Southern France. The herb flowers between July and September, and the flowers occur in whorls of 6-10 as terminal spikes of verticillasters. The fresh flowers contain 0.5% of volatile oil consisting chiefly of linayl acetate, linalool, gerniol, cineole, limonene and sesquiterpenes. Martindale 27th Edn., p. 1019.

DESCRIPTION

Macroscopical: Inflorescence is a terminal spike, flowers arranged in verticillasters arising from the axil of a rhomboidal bract. Individual flowers up to 5mm in length, 1-2 mm wide, bluish-violet to pale-brown in colour, calyx tubular and ribbed fine-toothed and pubescent, shining oil glands visible amongst the hairs; corolla purple-grey, tubular and two-lipped, posterior lip having two lobes and the anterior one three lobes. Four stamens exserted from the hairy throat of the corolla. Occasional leaf fragments up to 2 cm in length and 2-3 mm wide, dark-green to pale-green in colour, oblanceolate-linear, prominent midrib on the under surface.

Microscopical: Grey-blue powder, fragments of calyx, elongated epidermal cells with wavy anticlinal walls, covering trichomes multicellular, branched and frequent, occurring in a dense mat. Encapsulated labiate oil glands; corolla fragments, almost oval slightly wavy-walled epidermal cells, labiate glands and branched covering trichomes; glandular trichomes, unicellular stalk, papillose towards the apex, terminating in a single-celled glandular head; pollen grains spherical to ellipsoidal, 24-30 μm in diameter, 6 furrows and 6 pores, lines of pits radiating from the poles. Leaf fragments, almost straight-walled epidermal cells, covering branched trichomes and labiate oil glands, glandular trichomes, unicellular stalk and a bicellular head; bundles of narrow fibres and vessels from the midrib.

Total Ash: Not more than 8%.

Acid Insoluble Ash: Not more than 2%.

Thin-Layer Chromatography: Hörhammer, L. and Richter, G. (1963) Dtsch. Apoth-Ztg, *103,* 1737.

THERAPEUTICS

Action: Carminative. Spasmolytic. Antidepressant. Antirheumatic. Oil – rubefacient.

Indications: Flatulent dyspepsia. Colic. Depressive headache. Oil – (topically) rheumatic pain.

Specific Indication: Depressive states associated with digestive dysfunction.

Combinations used: May be combined with Rosmarinus, Avena and Cola in depression: with Cypripedium and Valeriana in migrainous headache: with Filipendula and Cimicifuga in rheumatism. The oil may be used in combination with Oil of Gaultheria as a liniment in myalgia or intercostal neuralgia.

ponins would be very dangerous, but taking them orally, as prescribed by a medical herbalist, is perfectly safe. Sarsaparilla (*Smilax officinalis*), which is rich in saponins, forms the basis of a wide range of non-alcoholic drinks. Within herbal medicine it is often used as an anti-inflammatory agent, particularly in the treatment of rheumatoid arthritis.

There are two main groups of saponins: steroidal and triterpenoid. The steroidal saponins are found in families such as the Dioscoraceae, Solanaceae and Liliaceae. Being most common in the monocotyledonous families, they are overall less widely distributed than the triterpenoid forms. They have a very similar structure to vitamin D, cardiac glycosides and steroid-based hormones. Steroidal saponins of *Dioscorea villosa* (wild yam) have provided the starting point for the commercial synthesis of several of the sex hormones.

Triterpenoid saponins are common in many dicotyledonous families and, unlike the steroidal forms, are relatively rare in the monocotyledons. They can occur in appreciable amounts; for example, the root of *Glycyrrhiza glabra* (liquorice) may comprise up to 15 per cent glycyrrhizic acid (with glucuronic acid as the sugar component), together with a similar amount of glycyrrhizin (the potassium and calcium salts of glycyrrhizic acid, which gives liquorice its sweet taste). The seeds of *Aesculus hippocastanum* (horse chestnut) may contain up to 13 per cent aescin, where the sugar components comprise two glucose molecules, glucuronic and tiglic acids.

Cardioactive glycosides

Ever since Withering used the foxglove (*Digitalis purpurea*) as a treatment for dropsy in 1785, there has been a lot of interest in the cardioactive properties of this genus within both herbal and allopathic medicine. Interestingly, Withering was unaware of the link between dropsy and heart failure when he first used this plant. Nowadays, it is the cardioactive glycosides extracted from the leaves of a number of different Digitalis species that are used. The principal glycosides of *Digitalis lanata* are digoxin, digitoxin and lanatosides A–E. The glycosides from this species have been found to be more rapidly absorbed from the gastrointestinal tract than those of *Digitalis purpurea*. Also, because of a slight difference in the site of acetylation in the molecule, they are more readily crystallized and therefore easier to extract commercially. Digoxin has become the most widely prescribed drug for congestive heart failure.

Convallaria majalis (lily of the valley) is widely used within herbal medicine for its cardioactive properties. Its effects are similar to those of Digitalis spp., but they are less cumulative. A large number of different glycosides have been identified, but the main glycoside is convallotoxin, which hydrolyses to form strophanthidin and rhamnose. In many respects cardioactive glycosides are similar to the saponins, as they also possess a steroidal aglycone component. There are two major groups: the cardenolides possess a five-membered lactone ring, whereas the bufadienolides have a six-membered ring. The glycosides of Digitalis spp. are cardenolides; their main action is on the myocardium, where the potassium-calcium ionic balance is altered so that potassium ions are lost from the cell and calcium ions are retained. This improves muscle contractility, and the outcome is a strengthening and an increase in efficiency. This is very effective in cases of congestive heart failure. To counteract the loss of potassium ions, their action is usually supported by administration of the potassium-rich *Taraxacum officinale* (herba).

The bufadienolides have a much more restricted distribution than the cardenolides; they are found mainly in the Liliaceae and the Ranunculaceae. In terms of therapeutic applications they are not as valuable as the cardenolides, since they would need to be administered in relatively high doses to bring about equivalent results. Such doses would not be practicable, owing to the highly undesirable side effects.

Cyanogenic glycosides

Plants rich in these molecules are potentially toxic, since their hydrolysis results in the formation of hydrogen cyanide. The presence or absence of this compound was recognized to be an important taxonomic feature early on in botanical studies; in the 1830s, Lindley used it to separate out rose subfamilies. It continues to be a major feature of plant taxonomic research

Interestingly, cyanogenic glycosides are found in very high amounts in cassava (*Manihot utilissima*), which forms the staple diet of many South American countries such as Columbia, and it must therefore be boiled carefully for a long period. Cyanogenic glycosides also found in appreciable quantities in the stone fruits, such as peaches, plums and apricots, etc. They are very useful therapeutically in low doses, as they are antispasmodic and sedative. Both these actions can be seen in *Prunus serotina* (wild cherry bark), which is a highly effective antitussive. It contains prunasin, which on hydrolysis yields glucose, benzaldehyde and approximately 0.1 per cent hydrocyanic acid.

Bitters

Members of this group, which includes those substances that stimulate the bitter receptors of the tongue via an intracellular change, are chemically very diverse. The largest chemical group of bitters is the triterpenoids; for example, the iridoids of *Gentiana lutem* (yellow gentian). This species is a common constituent of allopathic preparations, especially in the form of alkaline gentian. *Artemisia absinthium* (wormwood) is a particularly bitter-tasting herb, and this is due to its sesquiterpene content. The appetite-stimulating principles of such plants have been well known throughout history, and several have been incorporated into aperitif drinks such as angostura bitters and vermouth. Perhaps the best-known spirit containing wormwood is the one named after it − absinthe, which was originally made by steeping wormwood and other herbs such as *Hyssopus officinalis* (hyssop) in ethanol. After a long absence, it is to be reintroduced to the United Kingdom in time for the Millennium celebrations. It was originally imported into France from Switzerland by Henri Louis Pernod in 1797, and was soon adopted by the contemporary literary and artistic set. Its hallucinatory effects were legendary, and ultimately contributed to it being banned in France, Switzerland, Belgium and the United States just after the First World War. Traditionally brewed beer also has a bitters component in the form of *Humulus lupulus* (hops). This herb is frequently prescribed by today's medical herbalist.

The action of bitters is highly complex, so they have many possibilities as therapeutic agents. Their appetite-stimulating properties make them appropriate for any condition where appetite is decreased, and they also have a role in the management of anorexia nervosa. They increase the secretion of digestive juices, so the efficiency of digestion can be improved. In considering just one example, protein digestion, their importance can be illustrated. Normally, proteins are completely broken down to their constituent amino acids by protease action in the gut. If protein digestion is compromised, small polypeptides may escape into the bloodstream and become potential allergens. This is a well-recognized problem in cases of food allergy. In combination with a damaged ('leaky') gut wall, the opportunity for allergic reactions is further increased. It can therefore be seen just how important a role bitters may have by contributing to the breakdown of proteins into their constituent amino acids.

Bitters also promote bile flow, and their traditional use in this respect has been connected with improved liver function. Many argue that bitters are one of the most appropriate remedies for modern-day living, because more and more highly processed foods containing a variety of artificial additives are being ingested. This is an entirely separate consideration to that of the action of alcohol on the liver. These artificial chemicals will, of course, be metabolized by the liver. Any enhancement of liver function brought about by gentle stimulatory means, that is, a low dose of bitters, will provide a safe supportive action, and help prevent functional disorders. There is little doubt that the liver is now dealing with a far wider range of different chemicals than would be found in, for example, a pre-Second World War diet.

Alkaloids

These are unquestionably the most potent of all the chemical groups present. They are a diverse group of compounds that have always attracted a lot of research due to their marked effect on animal physiology. A large number of drugs are derived from alkaloids, their main effects being on the nervous and circulatory systems. They show a variety of pharmacological effects – analgesic, hallucinatory, vasoconstrictive, antispasmodic and locally anaesthetic.

The structure of alkaloids is highly variable, although most possess a heterocyclic ring that contains nitrogen. Generally speaking, they are crystalline substances that react with acids to form salts. They are usually bitter to the taste, caffeine being a familiar example. Other well-known examples include atropine, codeine, nicotine, morphine and strychnine; these examples exhibit a wide range of toxicity levels. As far as the herbalist is concerned, the presence of alkaloids in the list of a plant's constituents is not a cause for concern in itself since virtually every plant contains them to some degree. They occur either in their free states, as salts or as N-oxides, and would appear to act as an in-built defence against certain herbivores. Even so, the herbalist needs to be vigilant; accidental ingestion of a herb containing appreciable quantities of alkaloids will precipitate vomiting and diarrhoea. Since today's tinctures are mainly alcohol-based, extra caution is required, as alkaloids are more soluble in alcohol than in water. In earlier days, when aqueous tinctures were more commonly prescribed, they were unlikely to be present in very high amounts because they are only slightly soluble in water.

The tropane alkaloids

There are several alkaloids of therapeutic interest in this group: atropine, hyoscyamine, and hyoscine (scopolamine). These three compounds are restricted to one family – the Solanaceae, which includes species of Atropa, Datura, and Hyoscyamus. Interestingly, derivatives of some of the tropane alkaloids have become routinely prescribed in allopathic medicine, for example hyoscine butylbromide (Buscopan).

The leaf of *Datura stramonium* (thornapple) contains up to approximately 0.5 per cent alkaloids, mainly hyoscyamine and hyoscine, with a small amount of atropine. The leaves of *Atropa belladonna* (deadly nightshade) contain up to 0.6 per cent alkaloids, the main one being hyoscyamine, and the roots contain slightly more (up to approximately 0.8 per cent). *Hyoscyamus niger* (henbane) leaf has a much lower alkaloid content (again mainly hyoscyamine and hyoscine) of up to approximately 0.15 per cent.

Quinoline and isoquinoline alkaloids

As the name suggests, this group includes quinine and other alkaloids found in the bark of *Cinchona officinalis*. They are all derived from the amino acid phenylalanine. Examples derived from isoquinoline include morphine, codeine and papaverine (from *Papaver somniferum*), hydrastine (from *Hydrastis canadensis*) and berberine (from Berberis spp.).

Pyrrolizidine alkaloids

In terms of therapeutic applications, this group of alkaloids is not important. However, they are present in appreciable amounts in plants of the genus Senecio, and ragwort has posed toxicity problems for grazing animals. They are also present, albeit in small amounts, in some plants that are used in herbal medicine – for example, *Symphytum officinale* (comfrey). It is this fact that has placed these herbs under suspicion in cases of human hepatotoxicity, since the alkaloids break down to pyrrole esters, which are strongly alkylating and give rise to cell necrosis.

Ephedrine

This is an example of a non-heterocyclic alkaloid, derived from phenylalanine. Various species of Ephedra (Ma Huang) are used as a source of the alkaloids ephedrine and pseudoephedrine. The ephedras contain up to about 2 per cent alkaloids; in herbal medicine, *Ephedra sinensis* is prescribed for the relief of asthma and hay fever. Its effect is more lasting than that of adrenaline, and an additional advantage is that it is highly effective when administered orally.

Tannins

These are highly complex polyphenolic compounds, which possess the ability to coagulate proteins – hence their use in tanning animal hides. In herbal medicine this astringent property can be very valuable therapeutically, and tannin-rich plants are frequently used in the treatment of enteritis and diarrhoea, mouth infections and haemorrhoids. They are polar molecules and are therefore very poorly absorbed from the gut, although some breakdown products (tannates) have been found in the plasma. These are safely removed by the kidney during ultrafiltration, and it has been suggested that they may even have a beneficial astringent action on the epithelial cells as they pass along the tubules to the ureter. Owing to their coagulatory effect on proteins, it is generally recommended that herbs high in tannins should not be prescribed over long periods since they could interfere with the action of digestive enzymes. However, in the light of the average level of ingestion of tea, herbal medicine would not appear to be the main source of tannins for most patients. There are two main groups of tannins: hydrolysable and condensed. The former group is divided into two subgroups, depending on the acid derived on hydrolysis. Those tannins that yield gallic acid are termed gallitannins, and sources of these include *Hamamelis virginiana* (witch hazel) and *Aesculus hippocastanum* (horse chestnut). Tannins that yield ellagic acid on hydrolysis are termed ellagitannins, and the bark of *Quercus robor* (oak) is particularly rich in these.

Condensed tannins are far more resistant to hydrolysis, and hence the alternative name, non-hydrolysable tannins. Species with bark that yields condensed tannins include *Salix alba* (white willow), *Hamamelis virginiana* (witch hazel), *Cinchona officinalis* (cinchona) and *Quercus robor* (oak). Condensed tannins are not restricted to bark; they can also occur in the leaves of some species, including tea (which also contains hydrolysable tannins), *Agrimonia eupatoria* (agrimony), *Euphrasia officinalis* (eyebright) and *Potentilla erecta* (tormentil).

Mucilages and pectins

Plant mucilages are mixtures of polysaccharides that only partially dissolve in water to form viscous colloidal systems. Owing to their extremely high molecular weight, they are not absorbed into the bloodstream. Within herbal medicine, plants that have a high level of mucilages are of great importance in treating inflammation of the gastrointestinal tract, and any condition where the epithelium has become damaged. On ingestion they form a thin protective coating over the surface mucous membranes, and thus prevent irritant substances reaching the cells' surface, allowing healing to proceed. The most important herb in this group is *Ulmus fulva* (slippery elm), the inner bark of which has been used throughout the ages to treat a wide variety of digestive disturbances. It is non-toxic, and this is illustrated by the fact that it was once used as a weaning gruel by North American Indians. The small amounts of monosaccharide and disaccharide sugars provide easily digested substances. Although it is rarely used topically nowadays, it was once used in poultices to alleviate the pain of severe bruising and encourage healing.

In general, mucilages need to be extracted in cold aqueous infusions, since alcohol and high temperatures tend to destroy their molecular structure. Thus, *Ulmus fulva* is best given in powdered or tablet form, rather than as an alcoholic tincture. On contact with the aqueous medium of the stomach, the dry herb will start to form the characteristic mucilage. Because mucilages are neither hydrolysed nor absorbed during their passage along the gut, they can exert their therapeutic effect along the whole of its length.

Anthraquinones

For centuries, plants yielding anthraquinones have been valued as purgatives. There are several derivatives of anthraquinone, including anthrone, oxanthrone, anthranol and dianthranol. These have been extracted from a variety of plant families, where they usually occur as glycosides. In general, the anthracene purgatives are stimulatory to the colon and are thus indicated in persistent constipation; they act by increasing peristalsis. Interestingly, they work when the whole glycoside, rather than the isolated aglycone component, is presented to the gut. On hydrolysis, the glycoside components are absorbed separately, and the aglycone component thus reaches the colon wall via the systemic circulation. In addition, they will not bring about their effect in the absence of bile. The aglycone will exert an effect when injected, but not on oral administration.

The leaves or seed pods of senna (*Cassia senna*) were first used by the Arabian physicians of the ninth century. The active constituents are found in the pericarp of the fruit, and senna tablets BP consist of a powdered preparation of this. Even though a wide range of synthetic laxatives is available, senna remains one of the most important laxative agents. It is suitable for occasional use, or for habitual constipation.

Phenolic compounds

These compounds are very widely distributed in the plant kingdom, and also occur widely as glycosides. Salicin is probably the best-known glycoside. It can be extracted from Salix species (willow), and yields salicyl alcohol and glucose on hydrolysis. Gaultherin from Gaultheria and Betula yields methyl salicylate and primeverose; it was *Gaultheria procumbens* that was the natural source of oil of wintergreen, although nowadays it is extracted from a different species (*Betula lenta*). Vanillin is a phenolic aldehyde derived from the pods of *Vanilla fragrans* and other species; it was first described by the Spaniards in Mexico, and it is mentioned in the *London Pharmacopoeia* of 1721.

Coumarins

Coumarins occur naturally either in their free state or as glycosides, and many are phenolic compounds. Over 1000 different coumarins have been described. The fruits of *Apium graveolens* (celery) contain a variety of different coumarins, as well as furanocoumarins. They have traditionally been used in the treatment of rheumatoid arthritis, and are still regularly prescribed today in the form of a tincture. Another herb commonly prescribed by medical herbalists is *Angelica archangelica* (angelica), which also contains appreciable amounts of furanocoumarins and their glycosides. Both angelica and celery are members of the family Umbelliferae, which is particularly abundant in coumarins.

Volatile oils

With respect to their major therapeutic actions, in their extracted state these are mainly the domain of the aromatherapist. However, since they are present in so many different species and are occasionally prescribed by medical herbalists, they cannot be excluded. As noted in Chapter 6, they are now being assessed as alternatives to antibiotics because their high lipid solubility means that they can rapidly enter pathogens. In terms of chemical composition, they are highly complex mixtures of hydrocarbons and oxygenated compounds derived from the latter. The odour and taste usually originate from these derivatives rather than from the long chain hydrocarbons. As their name suggests, volatile oils can be extracted using steam distillation. Terpenes are the most commonly occurring hydrocarbons, and several groups are represented, including monoterpenes, sesquiterpenes, diterpenes and polyterpenes. Sesquiterpenes have been well researched; the azulenes and chamazulenes of *Matricaria recutita* (German chamomile) give this species its marked anti-inflammatory effects. However, they are not present in the natural state, being produced from volatile precursor molecules. It is thus essential to prepare aqueous infusions of chamomile correctly – that is, in a closed vessel (teapot) – to prevent these vital volatile components from escaping. Other chemical groups found in volatile oils include aldehydes, ketones, phenols, esters and peroxides.

To isolate or not to isolate?

In vivo activity is not only greater than the sum of the actions of the substances identified on chemical analysis, but it may also be different. This is because many of the individual constituents are chemically altered prior to absorption. *In vitro* experiments frequently fail to take account of this and, consequently, their conclusions are flawed. Often it is found that *in vivo* studies involving mice and similar species are administered the substance under investigation directly into the bloodstream (i.e. by injection), when in fact the herbal preparation is taken orally. When a particular compound in a plant acts as a prodrug rather than the actual active principle, then a thorough understanding of the chemical change(s) that the substance may undergo from the time that it is ingested until the time that it is absorbed in the small intestine is essential. Different pH levels, enzymes, and symbiotic bacteria in various regions of the gastrointestinal tract may cause several structural modifications of the original substance.

One of the best-known examples of plant-derived prodrugs is salicin, found in a variety of species including *Salix alba* (white willow). Salicin is a phenolic glycoside, which can be hydrolysed to form the substance that we know to be the active principle, salicylic acid. This was first extracted from willow bark in 1860, yet it was Edward Stone in 1763 who had first reported that an extract of willow bark was useful in reducing fever. Isolated salicylic acid is a very effective analgesic and antipyretic, but when taken orally it has a very unpleasant taste and is irritating to the gastric mucosa. Thus chemists sought to reduce these undesirable side effects, without reducing its therapeutic actions. The first simple modification was to neutralize the acid. The sodium salt, sodium salicylate, was first produced in 1875. Although this was more palatable, it still irritated the stomach lining. Another form was produced in 1886; this was phenyl salicylate, which passed unchanged through the stomach (and thus was not irritant) but became hydrolysed to phenol as well as the desired salicylic acid in the small intestine. Because phenol is toxic, this was soon abandoned. Acetylsalicylic acid was first introduced in 1899, and called 'Aspirin' by the Bayer drug company. It soon became the fastest selling drug in the world. However, the problem of minor haemorrhaging from the gastric mucosa still remains, and there have been several attempts to overcome this – for example, the introduction of coated slow-release forms that delay release of the salicylic acid until it reaches the small intestine. The history of the development of aspirin provides an excellent example of how striving to isolate an active principle known to have certain medicinal properties may result in obtaining the compound in a form that proves to have one or more unpleasant or even dangerous side effects. A valuable lesson can be learned by returning to the original extract of willow bark. This is found to contain salicin, which when ingested is modified by the symbiotic bacteria of the gut and is also chemically altered by enzymes found in the blood. In both cases, the product is salicyl alcohol (saligenin). The latter is oxidized to the active principle salicylic acid by enzymes in the blood as well as in the liver and other tissues. Because salicylic acid is only produced after absorption, it is not present in the gut, where it is so irritant. Thus, administering salicylic acid as its prodrug (salicin) would remove all the undesirable side effects. This is the principle adhered to when medical herbalists prescribe a tincture of *Salix alba*.

Salicin is especially effective in the treatment of chronic inflammatory conditions. Studies comparing the absorption of salicylate following administration of sodium salicylate and salicin reveal interesting results. The eight-hour plasma salicylate levels achieved after ingestion of sodium salicylate are found to be approximately one-half those obtained with salicin; thus, where sustained high levels of an anti-inflammatory agent are required, salicin is far superior to the sodium salt. Because the initial sharp rise in plasma levels is virtually the same in both, salicin may also be prescribed for more acute action.

It is a frequent finding in herbal medicine that the form in which a particular molecule occurs naturally, for example a glycoside (in combination with a sugar molecule), is far more easily dealt with by the body and is less likely to bring about undesirable side effects. This is probably related to the fact that, in their natural habitats, herbivorous and omnivorous animal species would regularly be ingesting a range of plant-derived compounds presented as, for example, glycosides. It is the aglycone (non-sugar) components of glycosides that often exhibit important physiological activity. Thus, when hydrolysed in the gut during digestion, the sugar component would be separated from its aglycone partner, creating two separate compounds with different properties.

The anthraquinone laxatives

As has already been noted in the biochemistry section, laxatives such as senna leaf are very commonly prescribed. Their action is complex, and it is interesting to note that the whole glycoside, although active when taken orally, is inactive if administered intravenously. Conversely, if the aglycone is isolated, it is active when given intravenously but devoid of activity if it is given by mouth. Thus it may be concluded that passage through the gut is a key part of the Pharmacokinetics of the anthraquinones. This is why, even in allopathic medicine, senna is given as whole senna leaf, rather than as an isolate of its components.

The sennosides of senna travel through the digestive system, and undergo progressive polymerization; as the molecules increase in size, they become inactive. Since a very large proportion (up to 90 per cent) of the sennosides end up in this inactive form and are excreted in the faeces, this leaves only a small amount to undergo conversion to sennidins and rhein-anthrone (Ling-Peschlow, 1992), which is brought about by symbiotic bacteria in the large intestine. They are therefore pharmacologically highly active at relatively small concentrations. The rhein-anthrone is the compound that stimulates peristalsis and inhibits water absorption in the colon, thus producing the laxative effect. Because the laxative action is dependent on the activity of the symbiotic gut flora, this becomes a very important factor in anthraquinone activity. It also explains why people show such a wide range of responses to these compounds. If the ecology of the gut flora has been disturbed in any way, for example following the administration of a course of antibiotics, then their response to the sennosides will be reduced.

The actions of medicinal herbs

Having reviewed the main chemical constituents of medicinal herbs, it is also relevant to consider their actions. In older reference texts, a wide range of terms is used to describe the way in which a particular herb acts. Although some of these terms are now obsolete, many are still in common usage, and a selection of these is outlined below; several will be familiar since they are also used to describe the action of orthodox drugs.

Anticatarrhals

Anticatarrhal herbs reduce the rate of production of mucus. The most obvious use is within the respiratory system, although they do exert effects within other systems. This action is usually associated with the tannin content of the herbs involved. Examples of anticatarrhal herbs include *Sambucus nigra* (elderflower) and *Hydrastis canadensis* (goldenseal).

Anti-inflammatory herbs

Several groups of herbs have an anti-inflammatory action as their main effect, including those high in salicylates such as *Filipendula ulmaria* (meadowsweet) and *Salix alba* (white willow). The latter is particularly effective in the reduction of the inflammation associated with rheumatoid arthritis. Other groups have a steroid-like action, for example *Glycyrrhiza glabra* (liquorice) and *Dioscorea villosa* (wild yam). One of the most widely used anti-inflammatory herbs in modern practice is *Matricaria recutita* (German chamomile), which has a marked action on the gastrointestinal system and is especially appropriate for children.

Antimicrobials

The term 'antimicrobial' was originally used to describe those herbs that either destroyed the causative organism directly, or acted to increase the body's ability to fight infection by strengthening the immune system. Thus herbs in this category can be further subdivided into antifungal, antiviral, antibacterial, antiparasitic or immuno-stimulatory groups. Perhaps the most widely used herb in this category is *Echinacea angustifolia* (or *Echinacea purpurea*). Although it does possess direct antibacterial and antiviral actions, it is best known for its stimulatory effects on the immune system. It is a very versatile herb, which can be taken internally or used as a topical application in the treatment of boils and other skin infections.

Antispasmodics

Antispasmodic herbs all relieve spasm in smooth muscle. The key herb in this category is *Viburnum opulus* (cramp bark). As its common name indicates, it has been used for centuries successfully to reduce muscular tension. The two main sites where these herbs are used are the smooth muscle of the gut (in conditions such as irritable bowel syndrome) and the myometrium of the uterus (in dysmenorrhoea).

Astringents

Astringent herbs have a binding effect on mucous membranes due to their action on the constituent proteins. The herbs in this category are usually high in tannins, and their range of action is very wide. They can be used to reduce bleeding from capillaries, to reduce inflammation or to inhibit diarrhoea. *Quercus robor* (oak) and *Geranium maculatum* (American cranesbill) are two species particularly rich in tannins. Today they are most commonly used in the treatment of diarrhoea or (externally) for haemorrhoids, and as a gargle in tonsillitis. *Hamamelis virginiana* (witch hazel), which is a powerful astringent, is one of few remedies available in liquid form as an allopathic preparation (albeit in the distilled form). It is highly effective in reducing inflammation and, if applied immediately following a trauma, it will prevent serious bruising.

Bitters

The range of applications of this fascinating group has already been considered above in the section dealing with chemical constituents. They have no equivalent in allopathic pharmacy. Where this action is required, herbal remedies are utilized (e.g. alkaline gentian). The actions are centred on the digestive system, including the liver, and they have a wide range of applications. The two most commonly prescribed plants that have a predominant action as a bitter are *Artemisia absinthium* (wormwood) and *Gentiana luteum* (yellow gentian).

Carminatives

These herbs help to relieve the build up of trapped wind in the digestive system. The species involved all have high amounts of volatile oils, and many are well-known components of gripe waters for babies. Examples include *Mentha piperita* (peppermint), *Foeniculum vulgare* (fennel) and *Pimpinella anisum* (aniseed). It is relevant to note that these are all common culinary herbs, and others that are carminative in action include sage, thyme and mustard.

Cholagogues

All these herbs stimulate the secretion of bile. They are commonly also bitters, and in addition have a slight laxative action. There are several herbs in this group, but by far the most commonly prescribed are the root of *Taraxacum officinalis* (dandelion), and *Rumex crispus* (yellow dock).

Demulcents

Demulcent herbs are soothing to mucous membranes, being rich in mucilage. There is no direct allopathic pharmaceutical equivalent to this group, although glycerine is used in a similar manner. Herbs high in mucilage include the bark of *Ulmus fulva* (slippery elm) and the root of *Althaea officinalis* (marsh mallow). Both these species are particularly appropriate for the digestive system, since they exert their effect along the whole length of the gut. *Glycyrrhiza glabra* (liquorice) is often used to relieve discomfort in the upper respiratory system, and *Zea mays* (cornsilks) is very effective in the treatment of cystitis. The precise mode of demulcent action of the various species in areas other than the digestive system is an active area of research; the large molecules that comprise the mucilages do not pass into the bloodstream, so it is not known how they exert their action at these other sites. It has been suggested that it may be through a reflex-like action initiated in the gut.

Diaphoretics

These herbs all promote sweating; with reference to the history of herbal medicine, they are some of the earliest mentioned herbs. This is because it was considered at one time that all disease could be 'sweated out', and it was this aspect that Thompson concentrated on (Chapter 2). One of the best examples of this category is *Achillea millefolium* (yarrow), which acts by dilating peripheral blood vessels (and thus has a minor but useful secondary role in reducing blood pressure). Historically, it has been recommended as a tea to be taken regularly in fevers. In American herbalism, the key diaphoretic is *Capsicum minimum* (cayenne). It has a far stronger action than yarrow, and is also common in external applications as a rubefacient.

Diuretics

Traditionally, the category of herbs described as diuretics has included both herbs that are truly diuretic in action (that is, increase the output of urine) as well as those that have other beneficial effects on the urinary system. Thus, herbs that are anti-inflammatory and demulcent in action are also found in this group. The therapeutic value of herbs that combine such actions within the urinary system is obvious. The most efficient true diuretic is the leaf of *Taraxacum officinalis* (dandelion) – hence the apt common name for this herb of 'wet-the-bed' (French; *piss en lit*)! It is certainly comparable in effect to the drug frusemide. The leaves of *Agropyron repens* (couchgrass) and the tigmas (silks) of *Zea mays* (corn) act in a similar manner, although their effect is not as marked as that of dandelion leaves. A major advantage of using the latter as a diuretic agent is their high potassium ion content.

Expectorants

These are all herbs that aid the removal of mucus from the lungs. They act by reducing the viscosity of the mucus and relaxing any bronchial spasm. The best-known expectorant is *Tussilago farfara* (coltsfoot).

Hypnotics

Herbs in this category induce normal sleep, and help to relieve anxiety without unpleasant side effects. They do not possess addictive properties. Mild hypnotics include *Tilia europea* (lime blossom) and *Matricaria recutita* (German chamomile). Stronger remedies include *Passiflora incarnata* (passionflower), *Humulus lupulus* (hops), *Valeriana officinalis* (valerian) and *Scutellaria laterifolia* (skull-cap).

Laxatives

Most herbal laxatives act by stimulating peristalsis. Although they are all safe, as with any substance promoting peristalsis, they are not used longterm. Within herbal medicine they would only be used temporarily, as a change in bowel habit is best brought about by a change in diet. Perhaps the best-known example is *Cassia senna* (senna). This has a long history as a laxative, its action being brought about via its anthraquinone content.

Nervines

This is an old-fashioned herbal term used to describe those herbs that have a beneficial effect on the nervous system. Because they include several different types of action, they are divided into separate categories: nervine relaxants, stimulants and tonics. One of the most frequently prescribed herbs at Wapping Health Centre is *Avena sativa* (oats). This is simply because it is one of the best nervous system tonics available, and since so many different disorders involve the nervous system, it is a component of a large number of tinctures. It has often been described as a good 'food' for the nervous system, and indeed it is best taken as a 'food' in the diet (e.g. as porridge oats). Because it is so easily digested, it is excellent in cases of general debility. *Verbena officinalis* (vervain) is a good relaxant nervine, and is used to treat mild depression – particularly when the individual concerned has been subjected to a lot of stress. *Hypericum perforatum* (St. John's wort), well known for its use in depression, also belongs in this category. True nervine stimulants are very rarely used in modern herbal practice, although they may be indicated in certain forms of depression. *Cola vera* (kola) is an example of such a stimulatory herb with a moderately high alkaloid content (including up to 1.5 per cent caffeine).

Vulnerary herbs

This is another old-fashioned herbal term used to describe those species that aid healing of wounds. Several other categories overlap with this one; for example astringents and demulcents, as their actions also bring about more efficient healing. The best-known vulnerary is *Symphytum officinale* (comfrey). This herb contains appreciable quantities of allantoin, which stimulates mitosis and thus has an important role in cell repair and growth following injury. One of comfrey's common names reflects this; it is often called 'boneknit'.

Factors affecting the growth of medicinal herbs

There are many factors that contribute to the production of a crop of medicinal herbs. These factors will be the same as those affecting any plant, but the overall interest in this case is in the amount of the pharmacologically active constituents. Much research has been carried out regarding the best growing conditions for a variety of species.

The main environmental variables include temperature, rainfall, day length and altitude, and edaphic (soil-related) factors. Temperature is of great importance; although a particular species will have adapted to survival in its natural habitat, most will be tolerant of a range of temperatures. However, although tropical species can be reared in temperate climates, they are usually unable to withstand the winter minima. Diurnal variation in temperature has marked effects on growth in many species.

Rainfall is a complex factor, as its precise effects will depend on other environmental features such as soil structure. In light soils, excessively high rainfall will cause leaching of essential minerals. If lack of minerals becomes a limiting factor, then growth will be stunted. It is a common observation that healthy plants growing on sandy soil will yield low amounts of active constituents following a particularly wet season. Heavy soils present a different problem when there is high rainfall; due to poor drainage, they become waterlogged and the soil air spaces that provide oxygen for root respiration become filled with water. With restricted supplies of oxygen leading to reduced rates of respiration, less energy is available for active uptake, and this is the method plants use to absorb many minerals essential for healthy growth. Thus growth is again stunted, and many metabolic pathways are affected by the unavailability of certain ions. The result is a reduced level of active constituent.

Soil will have a major influence on crop quality. Plant species vary greatly in their soil requirements, so detailed knowledge of both the biology of the herb and the edaphic factors is essential. Particle size determines water-holding capacity. Larger soil particles will lead to better drainage, but poorer water-holding capacity. Conversely, smaller soil particles will lead to poor drainage, but good water-holding capacity. This could be advantageous in areas of low rainfall but, where rain is plentiful, water logging is a serious problem owing to the reasons mentioned above. It is a common observation that in species high in mucilages, such as *Althaea officinalis* (marshmallow), the mucilage content is far lower in soil with high water retention. This is because the plant uses the mucilage as a water-retaining feature, and less is required when water is plentiful. Soil pH will influence solubility of ions in the soil water and, therefore, availability of minerals for uptake by the plant. Should a particular mineral become limited, then biosynthesis of important compounds could be affected.

Plants must also be supplied with the correct light requirements, both in terms of sufficient intensity for photosynthesis on a day-to-day basis and of day length. It is well known that certain species will only flower when on either a 'short-day' or 'long-day' regime, depending on the genus.

Altitude often determines the growth habit of a plant, as well as the production of metabolites. *Cinchona succirubra* (the source of quinine and other related alkaloids) may produce good vegetative growth at low altitudes, but its alkaloid content is low compared with levels achieved when it is grown at high altitudes. Interestingly, the alkaloids of *Aconitum napellus* (aconite) show the opposite pattern; they decrease with increasing altitude.

Collection, drying and storing

Depending on the part of the plant concerned, a range of different substances will be encountered. Generally speaking, the shoot system is the most metabolically active; during appropriate climatic conditions, the leaves are the major site of photosynthesis and the formation of primary metabolites. These will then undergo modification to become secondary metabolites such as glycosides, which account for a large percentage of active principles within herbal medicine. The roots tend to be less metabolically active, although they are frequently the main sites of storage. Large, insoluble molecules such as starch and other polysaccharides tend to be deposited here, providing valuable resources for those biennials and perennials that have to over-winter. As may be appreciated, not only do the parts of the plant vary in biochemical composition, but the amount of active principle therein will also vary according to the time of year. It has long been recognized that the season, as well as the time of day, is important in deciding when a particular crop should be harvested. This was noted by early herbalists such as Culpepper, and is a reflection of the fact that the concentration of active constituents is not constant. There are both seasonal and diurnal variations in the precise nature of the compounds as well as in their concentration. For example, the ovary of *Papaver somniferum* (opium poppy) shows the highest levels of morphine about three weeks after flowering, although the levels of other alkaloids such as codeine and papaverine are higher earlier on. In the case of *Digitalis lanata* (foxglove), the first-year leaves have the highest total concentration of glycosides. However, the lanatosides that are important medicinally, and they do not peak until the second season, which is therefore when the plants are harvested.

Although each species has its own specific requirements, there are general guidelines for the collection of herbs for medicinal use. Where leaves are the part of the plant to be used in the preparation of a medicine, for example *Urtica dioica* (nettle), they should be collected just as the plant begins to flower. If the flowers are the parts to be used, for example *Calendula officinalis* (marigold), then they should be removed before they open fully. If parts of the root system are to be used, then they should be dug up as the aerial parts of the plant start to die down.

The final stage of preparation, namely drying, is of paramount importance. A good quality crop with high levels of active principles can be ruined by a poor drying technique. All moist material is liable to decompose due to the saprophytic action of fungi and bacteria, so it must be dried as soon as possible after harvesting. Decomposition is not the only problem. The tissues are metabolically active, and enzyme action may begin to alter the compounds present. Occasionally this action is encouraged as part of the preparatory processes if such chemical modification is required, for example preparation of the root of *Gentiana luteum* (yellow gentian) involves natural fermentation. Drying can take many forms; where the climate is suitable it can be done outside, but where it is either too cool or too humid, the herbs are placed in special drying sheds, where conditions can be precisely controlled. This has the advantage that drying can be very rapid, and the result is more uniform. Colour of leaves is usually preserved, as is the odour of aromatic species.

Once the plant material has been dried, it must be stored under the correct conditions. Air-dried herbs – that is, those stored in sacks, bales, paper bags etc. – will still retain up to approximately 10 per cent water; if they are allowed to absorb more from humid air, they will be liable to deterioration. Precautions also need to be taken to prevent attack by a variety of invertebrate pests.

References

British Herbal Pharmacopoeia (1983). British Herbal Medicine Association.
Ling-Peschlow, E. (1992). Senna and its rational use. *Pharmacology*, **44** (Suppl. 1), 1–52.

Suggested reading

Evans, W. C. (1992). *Trease and Evans' Pharmacognosy*. Balliere Tindall.
Sneader, W. (1997). The discovery of aspirin. *Pharm. J.*, **259**, 614–16.
Phytotherapy: herbal medicine in the twenty-first century. Proceedings of the Symposium of the College of Practising Phytotherapists, May 1997.

6

Toxicity issues

Dangerous herbs?

> Mickle [great] is the powerful grace that lies
> In herbs, plants, stones and their true qualities:
> For nought so vile that on earth doth live
> But to the earth some special good doth give,
> Within the infant rind of this weak flower
> Poison hath residence and medicine power.
>
> Shakespeare (*Romeo and Juliet*, II, iii)

Herbal medicine regularly has the spotlight turned on it regarding the toxicity of some of the plants used. In allopathic circles, it is common for a mention of the use of medicinal herbs to be met with an automatic reference to problems with toxicity − especially with regard to hepatotoxicity. It is, of course, a frequently quoted excuse for dismissing herbal medicine out of hand. Amongst the general public, the opposite view is prevalent; namely that herbs are 'safe'. However, neither of these extreme opinions can be considered realistic. The reasoned scientific viewpoint must be that any substance ingested in excess is potentially harmful. No plant material is exempt from this general principle.

Medical herbalists need to ensure that both GPs and the general public are accurately informed regarding the true situation − one important aim of this book. If a large percentage of practising GPs are not even aware of the differences between homoeopathy and herbal medicine, how can they offer a fair appraisal of the more detailed aspects of herbal medicine, such as toxicity issues? We must endeavour to examine any claims for toxicity in a balanced and scientific manner. Western herbal medicine has frequently been promoted as a 'safer' alternative to certain allopathic drugs. As previously outlined in the historical section, there were periods where mainstream orthodox medicine was following highly questionable practices such as blood-letting, and the use of certain heavy metals as 'drugs'. At that time herbal medicine was a decidedly safer option, and this helped its furtherence in the nineteenth century. But what of the situation today regarding the issue of toxicity?

Reports have appeared in medical journals regarding the toxicity and harmful side effects of various herbal preparations. The first point to note is that virtually all the cases documented relate to herbal products purchased over-the-counter, and not to herbal medications prescribed by a practitioner. However, such accounts still need to be evaluated by the profession if herbal medicines are to receive their rightful status. An example of such an article is that published in the *British Medical Journal* in 1989 (MacGregor *et al.*). In this, five authors discussed four case histories and concluded that herbal products were a causal factor in the patients' liver damage. It later emerged that only one of the four cases was personally known to them, and that detailed past medical histories of the other three were not investigated (Mills, 1991). None of these patients had consulted a qualified herbal practitioner, but rather had purchased 'Kalms' or 'Neurelax' tablets from a pharmacy or health food shop, where they are freely available. Weston *et al.* (1987) presented a brief account regarding a 13-year-old Jamaican boy with Crohn's disease, who presented with fever, abdominal pain, ascites, and hepatomegaly, and went on to develop veno-occlusive disease of the liver. These symptoms were attributed to the ingestion of comfrey tea, even though 'the exact quantities of leaves given and frequency of administration are unknown'. Although the patient had been taking medication over 2–3 years, no attempt was made to consider the possible side effects of the drugs involved, which included sulphasalazine. In the *British National Formulary* (BNF), it is recommended that those taking this drug should receive regular haematological and hepatic screening. However, because comfrey contains pyrrolizidine alkaloids, which are toxic at high doses, it was automatically implicated. The authors concluded that their report 'serves as a reminder that herbal as well as orthodox medicine may have serious side effects', yet they offered no firm evidence that comfrey was the causative agent in this particular case. On detailed examination of these cases, it is clear that no direct link between the herbs and hepatocyte injury can be demonstrated. The readers of the articles, however, did not have the benefit of all the facts and thus, as is often the case, were misled by incomplete and superficial investigations, which concluded that the herbal medications were 'unsafe'.

The source of the problem

Research into problems with the toxicity of herbal medicines reveals three main potential causes:

1. Herbal material that has been adulterated with toxic non-plant material, e.g. lead
2. Plant species of proven toxicity
3. Interactions between the herbal medicines and orthodox drugs or other substances.

It is commonly reported that some herbal medicines available over-the-counter contain 'toxic substances'. These are mainly Asian and East African preparations, for example 'Kushtay' tonics, in which oxidized heavy metals (including lead and mercury as well as arsenic, zinc and tin) have been found as adulterants. A recent project carried out by the Medical Toxicology Unit of Guy's and St. Thomas' Hospital Trust, London, looked at the potential toxicological problems associated with traditional remedies and food supplements (Ministry of Agriculture, Fisheries and Food, 1996). The information was studied by the Ministry of Agriculture, Fisheries and Food, who concluded that, overall, the remedies did not represent a significant risk to public health. However, the contamination of certain Indian and Chinese medicines was a cause for concern. In the case of plant species of known toxicity, there are many reports of adverse reactions – for example, Belton and Gibbons (1979) described five cases of poisoning due to ingestion of tea prepared from the fresh leaves of *Datura stramonium* (thornapple), which contains atropine, hyoscine and hyoscyamine. The recent publication sponsored by the Royal Pharmaceutical Society, *Herbal Medicine: A Guide for Healthcare Professionals* (Newall *et al.*, 1996) lists possible interactions between herbal medications and allopathic drugs. These are mainly either potentiations or antagonistic effects, and few are true interactions. One example would be reduced absorption of the antifungal ketoconazole in the presence of herbal material containing anti-cholinergic activity.

In the case of heavy metal contamination, all the products described are freely available over-the-counter. Strict quality control measures and import limitations would prevent such occurrences. In no way are these events connected with the professional practice of herbal medicine. The innumerable accounts of accidental poisoning by ingestion of home made teas prepared from the leaves of toxic plants are being used constantly to call into question the safety of herbal medicines. These cases are totally independent of, and irrelevant to, the practice of herbal medicine. Highlighting potential herb–drug interactions would be extremely useful if GPs were better informed about herbal medicine in general, and were directed to appropriate research – such as the above publication sponsored by the Royal Pharmaceutical Society (Newall *et al.*, 1996).

A detailed literature survey on the toxicity of herbal medicines reveals the continuous recycling of the same small group of case histories, indicative in itself of the small total number of examples to draw upon and the rarity of toxic effects. There are relatively few professional medical herbalists available to review much of the media's inaccurate portrayal of herbal medicine, which frequently relates to issues of toxicity. Thus, much of it escapes unchallenged. Because most members of the general public and the medical profession will not have made contact with these specialists, many will fail to recognize inaccurate and prejudiced views. Much attention is focused on the dangers of potential interactions between allopathic drugs and herbal medicine, and this is frequently quoted as a reason to avoid taking the latter when on a prescribed medication. However, any substance taken by mouth is available for interaction with drugs, including other drugs, foods and dietary supplements. These molecules share several features, including toxicity at high levels, the ability to modify certain physiological processes and the same intestinal route of absorption. The effects of drug–nutrient interactions can be very similar to the interaction between two drugs, leading to potentiation or antagonism. Since either the nutrient or the drug availability may be affected, there are implications for both the drug therapy outcome and/or the nutritional status of the individual. The interactions have long been recognized and accepted as part of the expected clinical effects (Mason, 1995a). One example is the interference in vitamin D metabolism by phenytoin and other anticonvulsants. Thus, vitamin D supplementation is routinely recommended for those on long-term anticonvulsant therapy. A comprehensive survey of diet and drug interactions is presented by Mason (1995a).

Wise to analyse?

Bearing in mind these facts, many of the comments regarding the potential interaction of drugs with herbs fail to recognize that a number of these interactions could be identified by examining the biochemical composition of herbs in exactly the same manner as if they were food items or dietary supplements. In any case, many of the species used in herbal medicine are the same as those used as food crops, for example *Apium graveolens* (celery), albeit in much higher concentrations than would normally be encountered in the diet. However, once these plants are used within the framework of herbal medicine they seem to assume a completely different image, deserving dismissal rather than scientific investigation. Although a very common food item, grapefruit juice has been the subject of detailed analysis and has been found to alter the metabolism of a range of different drugs (Bailey *et al.*, 1994). In particular, it increases the bioavailability of felodipine by several times when compared with water. If similar information about the tinctures used in western herbal medicine were disseminated more widely, particularly amongst general practitioners, there would be no grounds for unfounded criticism. Any possible interactions between the various components and prescribed drugs would then be common knowledge, rather than the subject of speculation, and appropriate preventative steps could be taken. Nevertheless, there needs to be more clinical research to the same depth as the work on grapefruit juice, which included a detailed biochemical analysis of the active ingredients. It is no longer justifiable to reject herbal medicine on the basis that herbs are of 'uncertain' composition, since the advancement of spectroscopic analysis has made information on the active principles widely available to all those who wish to learn.

Herbal versus orthodox

Highlighting the possible danger of herbal medications is all very well if it is fairly contrasted with the dangers of orthodox preparations. Liver and kidney damage are recognized side effects of many commonly prescribed allopathic drugs, but this obviously does not stop their being prescribed. Their benefits are considered to far outweigh any adverse side effects, and hence the adage 'no effect without a side effect'.

It has been recorded that approximately 3 per cent of all hospital admissions are due to adverse drug reactions, and 20–30 per cent of cases of severe hepatic failure are drug-induced (Ward *et al.*, 1997); it therefore cannot be denied that allopathic drugs are a major factor in liver disease, and their effects are well-researched. Some drugs have a well-known and thus predictable effect on hepatocytes – for example, paracetamol – and the toxic effects of such drugs are usually dose-dependent. Other drugs produce far more variable, and often unpredictable, effects, and this group of idiosyncratic reactions may occur over an extended period of several weeks or months. Acute hepatitis may occur in response to administration of a range of drugs, including isoniazid, methyldopa, phenytoin, sulphasalazine, tricyclic antidepressants and ketokonazole (Ward *et al.*, 1997). The type of damage produced is characterized by cellular breakdown due to direct cytotoxicity, with or without cholestasis. Chlorpromazine is a common cause of the latter, with an incidence of 0.5–1.0 per cent in those prescribed it for more than two weeks.

Chronic liver disease may also result. Fibrosis and cirrhosis can develop following persistent damage to hepatocytes and, because it is characterized by cellular degeneration, cirrhosis is normally considered irreversible and thus persists after the drug is discontinued.

The kidneys are also highly susceptible to drug-induced damage. Research would seem to indicate that approximately 30 per cent of cases of acute renal failure are attributable to the direct effects of drugs (Hems and Lee, 1997). Commonly prescribed examples such as non-steroidal anti-inflammatory drugs (NSAIDs), many of which are also freely available over-the-counter, may result in functional renal insufficiency, glomerulonephritis and several other renal disorders. They can cause damage by blocking production of vasodilatory prostaglandins, which are vital in protecting against reduced renal blood flow because they act in opposition to substances that bring about vasoconstriction. In such cases, patients are at increased risk if they also have conditions such as diabetes or congestive heart failure. NSAIDs have been implicated in 36 per cent of all drug-related cases of acute renal failure (Hems and Lee, 1997). A relatively common hypersensitivity reaction resulting in interstitial inflammation and, ultimately, damage to the kidney tubule, is acute interstitial nephritis (AIN). More than 70 drugs have been identified as capable of producing this condition, the most common examples being the NSAIDs and antibiotics. Acute tubular necrosis (ATN) most commonly results from a direct toxic effect of a drug on the tubule cells. However, necrosis may also be brought about by a serious reduction in renal blood flow, leading to ischaemic tubular cell damage. The aminoglycoside antibiotics provide a well-documented example of a group of drugs with known nephrotoxicity; they are estimated to cause acute renal failure in 10–30 per cent of patients prescribed them. Gentamicin is the most commonly implicated example. The precise action of these compounds is not clear, but it involves accumulation of the drug within lysosomes, which ultimately rupture. This releases high levels of aminoglycosides into the cytoplasm, which inhibit normal metabolic activity and disrupt the structure of other cell organelles. In general, in these examples, when the nephrotoxic agent is removed the kidney will recover normal function, although there are cases where permanent damage has resulted.

The prolonged use of certain drugs such as analgesics may lead to long-term deterioration in kidney function, with subsequent chronic renal failure. This problem was first identified in the 1950s with a study of the effects of phenacetin, which has now been withdrawn. Nevertheless, the problem still remains, and the combination of paracetamol with salicylate-based drugs, caffeine or codeine seems to precipitate problems with respect to nephrotoxicity, although once again the precise mechanism is unknown. Addiction to stimulant ingredients such as caffeine present in the compound analgesic has been suggested as a factor in overuse. Abuse of single-substance analgesics is rare. The problem with analgesics is a well-known one, and is complicated by the fact that a wide range of these drugs can be obtained in large amounts over-the-counter. However, pack size restrictions were introduced for over-the-counter sales of para-cetamol and aspirin from September 1998; both single product and combination formulas were affected, and a single purchase is now restricted to 16 tablets. However, pharmacists will be able to sell up to 100 tablets in 'justifiable circumstances'. In a press release on 23 August 1997, Mr Alan Milburn, Minister of State, explained that 'those who have regular or long term requirements can continue to purchase larger quantities of up to 100 tablets in a pharmacy without the need for a prescription'. In addition to these pack size restrictions, the products also now bear health warnings:

> 'Immediate medical advice should be sought in the event of an overdose, even if you feel well'.

A significant reduction in analgesic-related renal disease resulted when Canada, Sweden, and Australia banned the sales of compound analgesics, which are now only available on prescription. The US National Kidney Foundation has recently recommended that all compound analgesics and NSAIDs should carry a nephrotoxicity warning, and that compound analgesics should not be available over-the-counter.

Such examples of liver and kidney damage are hardly isolated occurrences, and yet they do not attract media attention. On the other hand, as seen above, isolated cases of liver damage that may have been caused by herbal medicines most certainly do. Why?

Over-reaction

It is a scientific fact that, within any given population, each individual will show genetic variation. This is a consequence of the unique nature of each person's genotype. For virtually every chemical substance, there will be a small number of individuals showing an extreme form of reaction – that is, hypersensitivity. This occurrence is a reflection of the normal distribution, which also illustrates why most individuals will show little or no reaction to the substance in question. Obviously some substances are identified as toxic when, again with reference to a normally distributed population, most individuals are harmed and even killed by exposure to that substance. However, whereas most people eat a range of foods without any problem, some show sensitivity to one particular type, such as tomatoes. That does not mean that the rest of the population should be advised not to eat tomatoes, but rather that the individual concerned is sensitive to a chemical compound in that particular fruit, and should therefore be advised to avoid eating it. Similarly, some individuals are allergic to certain detergents. Once again, these do not become the subject of a widespread ban, but simply represent a problem for those who are especially sensitive to one of the chemicals present.

The way in which we react to such problems recognizes that, with reasonable precautions, these substances can be freely handled by most of the population without serious risk to health. The same type of logic is applied to pharmaceutical preparations. Most of the population will not show an adverse reaction, but in some cases even commonly prescribed drugs (such as penicillin) may cause serious problems. The level of acceptance of side effects is set by the statistical results of clinical trials – and once a drug has satisfied these criteria, it is deemed safe when prescribed at the recommended dosage level. It does not mean that nobody will be harmed by it.

Herbs prescribed by a qualified medical herbalist are also safe; most do not come supported by data from countless clinical trials, but they do come with a long history of highly successful use. And herein lies the problem. Much of modern orthodoxy only recognizes its own measurements of clinical efficacy, such as double-blind trials. There is very little data available for herbs, since medical researchers are very reluctant to include herbs on clinical trials without prior proof of efficacy – or at least evidence of safety. Both the latter factors would be brought up in the initial considerations of an ethics committee, and long-standing historical use of a herb counts for very little indeed. Thus, herbal research at the clinical trial level is generally blocked. Similar rules do not apply to trials of new man-made drugs, which are actively promoted by the pharmaceutical industry. Bradley (1997) makes an interesting point in that the total number of patients involved in a clinical trial will not exceed a few thousand, yet the number of individuals required to identify rare but potentially serious or lethal side effects of a drug is at least ten times this. Also, the patients participating in a clinical trial will form a very different sample from those who will eventually be receiving the drug from their GP. For example, participants will not be receiving other drugs and/or suffering from a range of other conditions. As Bradley points out, far less is known about the safety of new drugs than about those that have been prescribed over several decades. Most herbs have been prescribed safely over several centuries, but even this does not make them candidates for large-scale clinical trials or studies. As pointed out in the chapter concerning research, this is undeniably linked to the fact that nobody can make money from whole-plant medicines because plants cannot be patented. The identification of individual compounds that could be used, for example, as antiviral agents is a very active research area, especially with reference to HIV, because these individual chemical substances can eventually be patented as new drugs. This has nothing to do with herbal medicine, since only whole plant preparations are used. Accordingly, many herbalists would say that research centred on the activity of isolates has completely missed the point. Sadly, today's environment of profit-led research will never allow us to appreciate the true efficacy of whole-plant medications.

If full-scale clinical trials of herbs were routinely allowed, it would soon be concluded that most of the species implicated in questions of toxicity are in fact quite safe when used at the recommended dosage levels. Trials would also reveal the true efficacy of herbal medications. It is hardly good scientific practice deliberately to seek out isolated examples of 'toxic' herbs, and then use these reports to call the whole of herbal medicine into question. If one were to apply the same methods to a commonly prescribed drug such as paracetamol, highlighting only the negative aspects, then people would begin to think twice about using it.

It is a fact that, in Britain, paracetamol is the cause of 100–150 deaths annually. It is also the direct cause of 30 000–40 000 referrals to hospital each year (Editorial, *Pharmaceutical Journal*, 30 August 1997). However, the highlighting of only the negative aspects of such a drug would be fairly criticized by the scientific community as being unbalanced because, when used safely, paracetamol is a very effective drug. The same logic should be applied to herbal medicine, but sadly it is not. There is much prejudice against the use of herbs in clinical practice, most of which is based on ignorance. Most of the adverse reactions to herbs recorded in case histories are simply hypersensitivity reactions, which will occur from time to time.

Safeguards

Few medical herbalists would disagree that there should be tight controls on the sale of herbal medicines. Over-the-counter remedies should always specify the amount of active principle present and maximum dosages. Generally speaking, however, the protection against overdosing is automatic because, for most products, the amount of constituent present is relatively low. This relates to the form that the herb is in – i.e. the dried herb, rather than the tincture. Paradoxically, this can be the root of another problem for the medical herbalist. Many patients say that they have 'tried herbal medicine', when in fact their experience of herbal medicine relates to the purchase of a herbal remedy from a health food shop. Not surprisingly, the majority of them conclude that it 'didn't work'. However, they haven't even begun to experience herbal medicine as offered by a qualified practitioner. Apart from anything else, the taking of the actual herbs is only a small part of the overall holistic approach to treatment, and herbal remedies taken without guidance cannot be fully effective. Just as anyone can walk into a local pharmacy and purchase a wide range of orthodox medicines such as analgesics and antihistamines with very little guidance, so it is with herbal products. The lack of guidance in respect of orthodox medicines has been recognized by professional bodies such as the Royal Pharmaceutical Society and, in larger branches of High Street chemists, pharmacists are on hand to give advice on the various products on sale. No such expert advice is available for herbal medications, and purchasers simply have to rely on the information provided on the packaging. The prescription of herbal medicines on a FP10 is a relatively new phenomenon: Wapping Health Centre has been contacted by major High Street chemists, who are often completely baffled by the composition of herbal tinctures. The Royal Pharmaceutical Society has acknowledged the growing interest in the use of herbal medicines by funding a specialist guide, *Herbal Medicine: A Guide for Healthcare Professionals* (Newall *et al.*, 1996), which is aimed at orthodox practitioners and pharmacists.

Dose control

Critics of herbal medicine often say that precise quantities of active principle are unknown because potency depends on several factors, such as plant genotype, soil conditions, state of the crop at the point of harvest, preparation methods and the possibility of adulteration. These points were discussed in further detail in Chapter 5. It is argued that doses of pharmaceutical preparations are identical, and thus the effects are more predictable and safer. However, this does not guarantee that the patient will use them safely. They may be used as the agents of suicide and, unfortunately, capsules and tablets are often very easy to take in large quantities.

It is fortunate that the bitterness associated with many herbal tinctures prevents the ingestion of large enough volumes to cause serious harm. Several herbs are emetic in high doses, which also limits the potential for harm. The very fact that they are liquids rather than solids is another advantage when considering the risks of overdosing. If tinctures containing Schedule Three herbs are being dispensed, then only small volumes are provided (see Chapter 5). This serves to prevent accidental overdosing when the patient decides to take 'an extra dose' of, for example, an analgesic tincture containing a potent herb such as *Gelsemium sempervirens* (yellow jasmine).

Variety is the spice of life

Not all people will react similarly to the same dose of a particular drug, and this is due to the genetic variation present in the human population. Such variation is a problem when trying to predict the effects of a particular drug. However, the variability represented in different batches of the same tincture is a highly positive feature, and can be used to great advantage. When considering the development of new antibacterial agents, plants have received much attention. The precise form and amount of the antibacterial substance will vary from crop to crop, and this phenomenon offers an enormous advantage when so many species of bacteria have become resistant to current antibiotics. Antibiotics do not exhibit any variation in their chemical structure, and the evolution of resistant strains of bacteria is therefore inevitable and purely a matter of time. The rate of production of mutant strains of some bacteria (and viruses) has become a serious cause for concern, and several researchers have predicted that it is only a matter of a few years before we have no chemical means of eradicating these organisms. Usually the pharmaceutical industry responds to such crises by lining up a series of new generation antibiotics, but there are none in preparation at present, and we are at least 10–15 years away from producing a range of novel compounds capable of eradicating such virulent organisms (Service, 1995). Such production could involve modification of known chemical structures, or concentrating on new targets within bacterial cell metabolism. A new 'post-antibiotic era' is being referred to by many microbiologists (Leanord, 1997). The situation has been brought about by the constant increase in the use of antibiotics, which acts to maintain the selective pressure on the causative organisms. This in turn increases the rate at which resistant individuals are produced; both the number of species becoming resistant and the number of drugs to which they show resistance are increasing. Between 1980 and 1991, there was a 45 per cent increase in the number of prescriptions for antibiotics. The fact that the highest increase in the number of prescriptions is for the quinolones, macrolides, and cephalosporins is a very serious cause for concern, because these particular antibiotics are normally reserved for treating the most serious life-threatening infections. Such a prescribing trend can only lead to further resistance (Davey *et al.*, 1996). Twenty years ago, *Haemophilus influenzae* was routinely sensitive to ampicillin. Now, approximately 25 per cent of this species are resistant. The organism has developed beta lactamase, an enzyme that disrupts the beta-lactam ring of penicillin, and the only way to overcome this is to make use of another chemical – i.e. a beta-lactamase inhibitor such as clavulanic acid. The problem of antibiotic resistance has led to increased morbidity and mortality as well as increased costs, both in terms of extended hospitalization and research.

Perhaps we should be exploring the possibilities of utilizing whole plant extracts, known to be high in natural antibacterial (and antiviral) substances. It is logical to counteract organisms that have the potential to become resistant with a type of agent that deters this by being of variable composition. It is this feature which, in the living plant, provides highly efficient antibacterial activity. It is interesting to note that patients who seek help from a medical herbalist following years of unsuccessful treatment using antibiotics for conditions such as recurrent cystitis do very well indeed using the appropriate herbal tinctures.

In France, the problem of increasing resistance to antibiotics has already been recognized, and essential oils are routinely used as an alternative to antibiotics (Burne, 1996). In the UK, although essential oils are used within aromatherapy, taking them internally is not the rule. It is now possible to test which essential oils are effective against pathogenic organisms by means of an aromatogram. Particularly important is the ability of several oils to kill methicillin resistant *Staphylococcus aureus* (MRSA), which is a serious problem in hospital operating theatres.

Taking oils internally has several advantages. They can balance the intestinal flora, which is so often seriously disrupted by repeated use of antibiotics. They do not necessarily show a direct antibacterial action; some may act by altering the chemical composition of the internal environment in such a way that it becomes unsuitable for the pathogen. In doing so, as the pathogenic organism dies out, the normal ecology is gradually re-established with its associated normal species composition. The disruption of the normal gut flora is undoubtedly a factor in many cases of IBS and related gastro-intestinal disorders. Likewise, repeated use of antibiotics to treat cystitis, especially when the causative organism has not been identified, can result in a vicious circle of recurrent cystitis alternating with thrush. As the ecology of the normal vaginal flora is continually disrupted, the niches of those species that are normally found there are filled by opportunists, including fungi such as Candida. Unless something is done to alter both the biotic and abiotic factors, these invading species will persist.

Toxic plants: the facts

The situation regarding the classification of plants in terms of a hierarchy of toxicity is very complicated. To simplify this, three working definitions may be set up, making a clear distinction between the following:

1. Herbs that are known to contain highly poisonous substances, and are therefore toxic when ingested even in very small amounts. Their use as medicines is strictly controlled under The Medicines Act (1968) – for example, *Atropa belladonna* (deadly nightshade).
2. Herbs that contain high amounts of chemical groups known to be toxic if ingested in large amounts. A maximum recommended dose reflects this – for example, *Symphytum officinale* (comfrey).
3. Herbs that are non-toxic even when ingested in large amounts, but in isolated cases may cause hypersensitivity reactions – for example, *Althaea officinalis* (marshmallow).

The very fact that herbalists are provided with maximum recommended doses for every herb in the *British Herbal Pharmaco-poeia* acknowledges that herbs cannot be the harmless plants that some patients assume them to be. Nor are they all highly dangerous agents, as some uninformed practitioners seem to presume. They are prescribed with the same detailed consideration with respect to biochemical composition and dosage as any drug.

There are many studies of the toxicity of individual plants used as medicines, but no detailed reviews relating solely to species used in western herbal medicine. However, a comprehensive survey of the toxicology of British plants was produced by the Ministry of

Agriculture Fisheries and Foods in 1984 (Cooper and Johnson, 1984). Their conclusion is that, although many plants are known to be poisonous, few species present a serious risk and cases of severe poisoning are rare. With regard to the plants included in the *materia medica* of today's medical herbalist, some are designated poisonous within the terms of the 1968 Medicines Act. Most of the herbs listed within this category are not available for general sale, although a small number can be purchased in preparations for topical use only. The remainder are only available on prescription from a medical herbalist or doctor. In general, this group of plants is only used rarely. A separate category includes those that are emetic in high doses – within this category only one, *Lobelia inflata*, is used routinely. It is lobelia's relaxant properties that are valued, rather than the harsher effects on the digestive tract that only occur when prescribed in high doses.

A scan of the literature reveals a limited amount of toxicological data for medicinal herbs. However, as mentioned above, there are certain constituents that are intrinsically toxic. By considering information provided by detailed biochemical analyses, it is possible to predict the potential adverse effects that may occur with some herbs. For example, the relatively high amounts of sesquiterpene lactones found in the Compositae means that some of the members of this plant family could precipitate a hypersensitivity reaction in susceptible individuals. Species that might be involved include *Achillea millefolium* (yarrow) and *Tanacetum parthenium* (feverfew). The furanocoumarins found in members of the Umbelliferae, such as *Apium graveolens* (celery) and *Angelica archangelica* (angelica), may precipitate a phototoxic reaction. Some species can provoke gastrointestinal irritation, which can be a result of a wide range of compounds. The anthraquinones of *Cassia senna* (senna) are often implicated (indeed it is these that result in the familiar laxative action). The saponins of *Polygala senega* (snakeroot) and the diterpenes of *Peumus boldo* (boldo) may also prove irritant.

Plants and cancer

Plants are both implicated in causing cancer and in protecting against it. Many herbs contain chemicals that are capable of stimulating cancer in laboratory animals, but this does not necessarily mean that these plants are dangerous when used as phytomedicines. Many food plants have been tested and found to contain naturally occurring carcinogens at levels of between 5 and 10 per cent of total dry weight. It is generally accepted by botanists that these toxic substances provide the plant with protection against herbivorous insects, as well as pathogenic bacteria and viruses. The fact that most people do not develop cancer following regular intake of these plants shows that humans must already have or must receive protection against this potential carcinogenic action. It is also the plants in their diet that provide this protection – for example vitamin C, vitamin E and beta-carotene are all powerful antioxidants. They are effective free-radical scavengers, and prevent damage to vital structures such as cell membranes. The body is exposed to ever-increasing levels of substances that are sources of free radicals; for example, pollutants such as nitrogen dioxide and cigarette smoke. The metabolism of many drugs results in the production of free-radical products (e.g. nitrofurantoin). Although there are endogenous enzyme systems that function to protect against such action, they are not capable of providing full protection. This, together with the fact that diseases such as atherosclerosis, Parkinson's (and other degenerative neurological disorders) and inflammatory bowel conditions involve free-radical damage has led pharmacists to consider recommending antioxidant supplementation (Mason, 1995b). However, there is little doubt that the best source of antioxidants is fresh plant material. One major advantage is that in this form they will be accompanied by minerals that the plant has absorbed from the soil. These contain the elements that are essential co-factors for endogenous antioxidant enzymes, including selenium, zinc and copper.

It has been demonstrated statistically that those people whose diets are high in foods containing large amounts of these substances exhibit a lower incidence of many forms of cancer. However, those who eat a diet low in antioxidant substances – for example, a diet consisting of a lot of 'junk' food and red meat but very little plant material – will show a correspondingly higher overall incidence.

Regulation of herbal medicine

With the growing market in herbal remedies, and renewed interest in herbal medicine in general, it has become necessary to review the status of the products available. At present, herbal remedies are available through a variety of outlets including supermarkets, health food shops, pharmacies and specialist mail order companies. They are available in a variety of forms, ranging from the raw product (i.e. the dried material) to tablets, liquid preparations, and capsules. In the UK, most herbal products come under the control of the Ministry of Agriculture, Fisheries and Foods (MAFF), since they are not accompanied by claims of medical efficacy. They are essentially on the borderline between foods and medicines and, because they are free of medical claims, the Medicines Control Agency is, at present, content for them to remain a special case and thus exempt from the legislation applied to medicines. This situation may well change now that EU directives are attempting to define more precisely just what a medicinal product is. Directive 65/65 EEC (Article 1) states that a medical product is:

> 'any substance or combination of substances presented for treating or preventing disease in human beings or animals,'
> and
> 'any substance or combination of substances which may be administered to human beings or animals with a view to making diagnosis or to restoring, correcting or modifying physiological functions in human beings or animals is likewise considered a medicinal product.'

The great majority of the herbal remedies on sale in the UK have been available for a very long period of time, and pre-date the Medicines Act of 1968. In 1971, all medicinal products, both allopathic and herbal, were issued with a Product Licence of Right (PLR). This was not preceded by a detailed investigatory exercise, and simply involved the manufacturers having to provide basic information about their products, together with evidence that they had been in existence prior to 1971. Any manufacturers applying for a Product Licence after 1971 have had to be assessed by the Licensing Authority (LA), who consider aspects of efficacy and safety. It was evident that these same standards must retrospectively be applied to pre-1971 items, and an EEC Directive required this to be completed by May 1990. A review was duly carried out, and the LA agreed to accept historical bibliographic evidence for efficacy. For most of the items involved it was obviously impractical to demand evidence via the implementation of clinical trials, and therefore it was agreed that a herbal medicine would bear a label which identified it as 'a traditional herbal remedy for the symptomatic relief of . . .'.

The label would also contain the advice: 'If symptoms persist, consult your doctor'.

However, it was considered that regulations must be stricter for those conditions where self-diagnosis could be dangerous, and therefore clinical trials would have to be carried out for this category of remedy. The MCA controls the use of medicinal products in accordance with The Medicines Act (1968), so all new licensed herbal products are assessed for safety, quality and efficacy. This is in full accordance with EU guidelines. The public still have free access to dried herbs and medicines prepared by herbalists, because these both come under an exemption in Section 12(1/2) and Article 2 (SI 1450) of the Medicines Order of 1971. Such items must be solely plant materials sold under their scientific names, with no claims or recommendations as to their medicinal use. The EU directive does require herbal medicines that are 'industrially' produced to have marketing authorization. However, after due consideration it was decided that the production of herbal medicines within the UK was not on a large enough scale to fall within this description, and such medicines are therefore currently exempt, although there is still much discussion as to how these products may be properly regulated.

Plants that are highly toxic are specifically controlled under The Medicines Act (1968), so that genera such as Digitalis are designated 'prescription only medicines' (POM). These are not available to the general public except via a registered herbal practitioner or doctor. Another 25 are regulated in Part One of The Medicines Order S1 2130 (The Retail Sale and Supply of Herbal Medicines), and these can only be supplied by a pharmacy. Part Two of the same Order deals with which species can be supplied by a registered herbal practitioner – for example, *Atropa belladonna* (deadly nightshade) and *Ephedra sinica* (Ma Huang). The third part of the Order deals with dosage and administration of the herbs.

WHO guidelines for the assessment of herbal medicines

The World Health Organization estimates that approximately 80 per cent of the world population use herbal medicine for primary health care (Farnsworth *et al.*, 1985). These medicines range from freshly collected herbs gathered by indigenous rural populations to standardized pharmaceutical preparations used in sophisticated modern medicine.

As part of its programme on traditional medicines, the WHO has produced a series of guidelines for the assessment of over-the-counter herbal products (WHO, 1991). The WHO defines herbal medicines as any 'finished labelled medicinal products that contain as active ingredients aerial or underground parts of plants, or other plant materials or combinations thereof, whether in the crude state or as plant preparations'. It also states that 'medicines which contain plant material combined with chemically defined active substances, including chemically defined isolated constituents of plants, are not considered to be herbal medicines'.

The WHO has played an active role in identifying and promoting safe and effective herbal medicines for use in primary health care, and has strongly supported the use of herbal medicines to promote the health of communities. In 1978, the Declaration of Alma-Ata provided for the use of proven herbal remedies in national drug policies. The WHO recognizes the growing interest in and demand for traditional herbal remedies; hence the development of the latest guidelines, which cover the pharmaceutical assessment, standards for crude plant material, the composition of plant preparations, stability of the final preparation, safety assessment, toxicological studies, activity and measurements of efficacy. Finally, there is a detailed set of guidelines for the labelling of herbal products.

Interestingly, the assessment makes the observation that 'as a basic rule, documentation of a long period of use should be taken into consideration when safety is being assessed. This means that when there are no detailed toxicological studies, documented experience on long term use without evidence of safety problems should form the basis of risk assessment.'

If such an open-minded view were taken of herbal medicine in general, much more research would have been allowed.

The European Union has developed a series of guidelines entitled *The Quality of Herbal Remedies* (EEC Directive, undated). They were produced in response to the general acceptance that there needs to be a standardization of herbal medicines, and are based on the WHO guidelines, providing outlines for labelling requirements and characteristics of the final product. The format provides headings for qualitative and quantitative composition, and for pharmacological properties including pharmacodynamic and pharmacokinetic aspects. Clinical headings include therapeutic indications, posology, contra-indications, special warnings, interactions with other medications, pregnancy and lactation, undesirable effects and overdose.

To further improve the status of herbal medicine and maintain high standards, the leading professional bodies of France, Belgium, the United Kingdom, Germany and Switzerland came together to form the European Societies Co-operative of Phytotherapy (ESCOP). At the centre of ESCOP's activities is the formation of a set of scientific monographs for the herbs used in phytotherapy. Fifty have been published to date, and others are in preparation.

This monograph system is well established in Germany, where herbal products are considered as a single active principle. Herbal medicines are very popular and are routinely used in mainstream medicine, so strict regulation is essential. This regulation is carried out by the German Federal Health Office, which clearly defines both details of the manufacturing process as well as the potency of the final product. The monographs are compiled under the auspices of the Ministry of Health Committee for Herbal Remedies, and approval of a new remedy depends on the presentation of considerable scientific data (Keller, 1991). There is much activity in terms of the preparation of scientific monographs, as it is recognized that this is the major way to move forward in terms of presenting the scientific front of herbal medicine. The WHO is currently producing 28 monographs, some of which overlap with those produced by ESCOP. In addition, the American Herbal Pharmacopoeia is producing monographs on several herbal medicines, and *Hypericum perforatum* (St. John's wort) has already been published (Upton, 1997). The United States Pharmacopoeial Convention is also producing monographs for inclusion in the *USP Drug Information Update*, which is an annual publication. To date, three herbs have been covered: valerian, comfrey and ginger.

The heart of the matter

Improvement in the legal regulation of herbal medicine will not in itself alter the personal prejudice of some. Perhaps the last word on the subject of the safe use of herbal medicine should come from Dr David Atherton, a hospital consultant:

> 'Most of all, everyone with a stake in the subject needs to remain conscious that the main aim of such [herbal] treatment is to relieve suffering safely. The opening of channels of communication in an atmosphere less pervaded by suspicion and hostility is an essential part of the process.'
>
> David Atherton, 1994

References

Atherton, D. J. (1994). Towards the safer use of traditional remedies. *Br. Med. J.*, **308**, 673–4.

Bailey, D. G., Malcolm, J., Arnold, O. and Spence, D. (1994). Grapefruit and drugs; how significant is the interaction? *Clin. Pharmacokinet.*, **26(2)**, 90–98.

Belton, P. A. and Gibbons, D. O. (1979). Datura intoxication in West Cornwall. *Br. Med. J.*, **1**, 585–6.

Bradley, C. (1997). How to evaluate a new drug in general practice. *Prescribers' J.*, **37(3)**, 158–65.

Burne, J. (1996). A spoonful of oil makes the medicine unwanted. *The Independent*, 30 January.

Cooper, M. R. and Johnson, A. W. (1984). Poisonous plants in Britain and their effects on animals and man. *Ministry of Agriculture, Fisheries, and Food, Reference Book 161*. HMSO.

Davey, P. G., Bax, R. P., Reeves, D. *et al.* (1996). Growth in the use of antibiotics in the community in England and Scotland 1980–93. *Br. Med. J.*, **312**, 613.

EEC Directive 75/318/EEC. Undated.

Farnsworth, N. R., Akerele, A. S., Bingel D. D. and Eno, Z. (1985). Medicinal plants in therapy. *Bull. WHO*, **63(6)**, 965–81.

Hems, S. and Lee, A. (1997). Drug-induced renal disorders. *Pharm. J.*, **259**, 214–19

Keller, K. (1991). Legal requirements for the use of phytopharmaceutical drugs in the Federal Republic of Germany. *J. Ethnopharmacol.*, **32**, 225–9.

Leanord, A. (1997). Antibiotics: What is the current position? *Practitioner*, **241**, 91–4.

MacGregor, F. B., Abernethy, V. E., Duhabra, S. *et al.* (1989). Hepatotoxicity of herbal remedies. *Br. Med. J.*, **299**, 1156–7.

Mason, P. (1995a). Diet and drug interactions. *Pharm. J.*, **255**, 94–7.

Mason, P. (1995b). Antioxidant supplements: should they be recommended? *Pharm. J.*, **254**, 264–6.

Mills, S. (1991). Are herbs safe? *Br. J. Phytotherapy*, **2(2)**, 76–83.

Ministry of Agriculture, Fisheries and Food (1996). *Toxicological Problems resulting from Exposure to Traditional Medicines and Food Supplements*. MAFF.

Newall, C. A., Anderson, L. A. and Phillipson, J. D. (1996). *Herbal Medicines: a Guide for Healthcare Professionals*. The Pharmaceutical Press.

Service, R. F. (1995). Antibiotics that resist resistance. *Science*, **270**, 724–7.

Upton, R. (1997). St. John's wort, *Hypericum perforatum*: Quality control, analytical and therapeutic monograph. American Herbal Pharmacopoeia.

USP DI Update (December 1997). The United States Pharmacopoeial Convention, Inc., Rockville, Maryland.

Ward, F. M., Daly, M. G. and Lee, A. (1997). Drug-induced hepatic disorders. *Pharm. J.*, **258**, 863–8.

Weston, C. F. *et al.* (1987). Veno-occlusive disease of the liver secondary to the ingestion of comfrey. *Br. Med. J.*, **295**, 186–7.

World Health Organization (1991). Guidelines for the assessment of herbal medicines. Geneva.

Suggested reading

Blumenthal, B. *et al.* (eds) (1997). *The German Commission E Monographs*. American Botanic Council.

D'Arcy, P. F. (1991). Adverse reactions and interactions with herbal medicines: Part 1. Adverse reactions. *Adv. Drug React. Toxicol. Rev.*, **10(4)**, 189–208.

Roe, D. A. (1989). *Diet and Drug Reactions*. Van Nostrand Reinhold, New York.

Shanahan, P. M. A., Thomson, C. J. and Amyes, S. C. G. (1994). The global impact of antibiotic-resistant bacteria: their sources and reservoirs. *Rev. Med. Micro.*, **5**, 1740–82.

7

What is the herbalist's therapeutic approach?

Doctors are men who prescribe medicine of which they know little, to cure diseases of which they know less, in human beings of which they know nothing.

Voltaire, 1694–1778

It is the aim of any practitioner to restore health. The World Health Organization defines health as 'more than the absence of illness, it is the **active** state of physical, emotional, mental, and social wellbeing'. This definition encompasses the same aspects of the patient's health that a herbalist will always take into account when recording a case history and formulating a treatment plan. It also reflects the holistic ethos of complementary medicine in general; attention to just one of these categories in isolation will not result in an effective approach to treatment, since all four areas are interconnected in a highly complex manner. Not only is the interaction very complex, but it varies from individual to individual, and depends on the particular medical condition being considered. Although one of these aspects may predominate, the others can never be left out of the equation.

Holistic medicine such as herbal medicine recognizes the total needs of the patient, rather than focusing on the disease process in isolation. Although the concept of holistic medicine is an ancient one, dating back to Hippocrates, the term 'holism' was introduced by Jan Christian Smuts in the 1920s in order to distinguish between the approach based on treating the patient as an individual and that based on reductionism. The reductionist approach is rejected in that it fails to recognize that the whole organism is greater than the sum of its parts, and that each organism is biologically unique. All individuals cannot, therefore, be expected to respond in a 'standard' way, and a treatment plan that takes account of this, and is truly individually tailored to a patient's needs, is bound to be more successful than one that has no flexibility.

In the nineteenth century, 'hospital medicine' was beginning to develop. Patients were removed from their home surroundings and placed in a specialized environment. Although this obviously had its advantages, it also meant that patients were removed from their normal habitat and their usual social contacts were altered or curtailed. With this development of hospital medicine came the advancement of laboratory science. These changes could only serve to promote the reductionist approach. Patients had become 'cases' under 'investigation'. It was all too easy to view the individuals as depersonalized objects removed from their natural environment. Whereas the doctor had always previously visited patients at home (treatment by a specialist being relatively rare), it now became possible to have medical care at specialist centres. The major advantage of the home visit was that it allowed the practitioner to assess a patient's living conditions, diet, etc., and now this had to be separately ascertained, by means of taking a detailed case history. Such aspects of lifestyle could be easily overlooked; institutionalized medical care did not lend itself to the holistic approach. It was simply not practical on a large scale.

Once established in hospitals, the reductionist approach became the norm within health care. The proponents of the 'old-fashioned' holistic approach were left on the periphery of western medicine; they became known as alternative practitioners, and became marginalized with respect to their utilization within the 'accepted system'.

Holistic medicine attempts to make treatment a two-way process. It acknowledges the responsibility of patients for their own health, and aims to reinforce their attempts to help themselves through education in matters such as diet, etc. This reflects the fact that the maintenance of good health is an active process rather than a passive state, as emphasized in the WHO definition. It also recognizes the capacity of the body for self-healing.

An ecological approach?

The ultimate aim of treatment by herbal medicine is to prescribe herbs which restore health by stimulating the body's own processes to work more efficiently. Just as an ecosystem is formed by the complex interactions between biotic factors (living organisms) and abiotic factors (environmental parameters), the human organism forms very complex interactions with the external environment. It is the interaction with that environment that provides potential for directly affecting those aspects of health mentioned in the WHO definition above; our physical state can be affected by many environmental factors, as can our emotional, mental and social well-being. On the other hand, our overall health status determines how we react to the outside world. It may be said that we need to be kept in balance with our environment. On another level, the whole organism must also be kept in balance to function efficiently. This is the basis of homeostasis, to which treatment by herbal medicine relates directly.

A healthy individual is one who is well balanced, both in terms of psychological outlook and physiological function. Disorders occur when functions of organs deviate from the norm, usually setting off homoeostatic mechanisms designed to restore the particular parameter to the normal level. Depending on the cause and severity of the shift away from normal, the body is self-healing via this homoeostatic regulation. Throughout the history of herbal medicine, this self-healing aspect of the body has been strongly acknowledged. It is a theme that is present in several other branches of complementary medicine, notably traditional Chinese medicine. Here, disease is seen as a state of disharmony, and the object of any treatment is to trigger the organism's natural tendency to achieve a state of balance. Thus healing is not viewed as an external force, but rather as an inherent capacity of the organism.

This idea is also encompassed by practitioners of osteopathy; Korr (1991) summarizes the practice of osteopathy as:

'The osteopathic physician sees it as his or her major responsibility to evoke and support those [homeostatic] mechanisms, to remove impediments to their functions. It is the patients who get well and not the procedure or the medication. Cure comes from within, a mechanism of the body's healing power.'

Those branches of complementary medicine that truly embrace the holistic ethos in their practice reject the reductionist approach that evolved following the period in history when there was extensive dissection of the human body. Although dissection was of vital importance, since it allowed a far greater understanding of human anatomy and physiology, it led to the development of a mechanistic model where the body was viewed as a series of separate components. Thus diagnosis came to adopt the same approach, and the patient was reduced to being thought of as a series of component parts (body systems). This is the so-called reductionist paradigm. In disease, a causal agent is considered to have interfered with the normal processes, so causing a 'malfunction'.

The practice of traditional Chinese medicine is based on a philosophy that differs dramatically in its central concepts. The idea that an organism is constantly changing and interacting with its external environment is summarized by Watson (1991):

'Although in constant flux, the system is self-regulating and has a natural tendency towards harmony and balance.'

Although western herbal medicine would fully embrace the above idea that an organism is constantly changing and interacting with its environment, it does not use the same reference point for the agent of the dynamic aspect of the organism, that is 'Qi' (the life energy or vital force). It is accepted, however, that disease is seldom caused by a single factor, but rather by a series of contributory factors. These may include a wide range of influences, such as emotional upsets, trauma, diet, fatigue, environmental pollutants, climatic conditions and social activities. Such considerations are rarely taken into account within mainstream medicine.

Background considerations

As far as the practice of modern western herbal medicine is concerned, it is difficult to define a common underlying philosophy. This is mainly due to its complex history, which involves a distillation of ideas from several different countries. However, most of today's practitioners have been trained in the physiomedical tradition, which evolved in North America in the second half of the nineteenth century. This acknowledges a vital force that directs the organism, and as such shares a link with traditional Chinese medicine. Physiomedicalism was established by Thompson (1769–1843), and further developed by Beach, Cook, Lyle and Thurston. The dominant theme of Thompson's work was that disease results in the accumulation of toxic substances, which must be removed. The central theme of his approach to treatment was therefore directed at promoting eliminatory processes such as diaphoresis and emesis. Other physiomedical concepts included the 'equalization of the circulatory system', developed by Beach (1859), and a consideration of the interplay between the nervous and circulatory systems, described by Cook in his publication *The Science and Practice of Medicine* (1879). The role of the nervous system was further developed by Thurston in his *Philosophy of Physiomedicalism* (1900), which considered in particular the effect of the autonomic nervous system on the state of individual tissues. Thurston's work was handicapped by his lack of knowledge of the effects of herbs at a cellular level. Histology was a relatively young science, awaiting the development of more sophisticated microscopes and staining techniques. His work relied on complex relationships between the nervous and circulatory systems, although he was unable to give accurate physiological details. The concept of cell receptor proteins was far in the future. However, this does not alter the fact that the most important aspect of his work, namely the classification of the various herbs according to how they acted, was well observed. Herbalists today are able to re-examine the work of the physiomedicalists and, in the light of scientific advances, appreciate just how accurate the work of Thurston and his contemporaries was.

Although each of these early pioneers chose to concentrate on one or two body systems and their role in the overall 'balance' of the organism, the unifying theme is what we refer to today as homeostasis. The early physiomedicalists summed up their role as one of trying to achieve an equilibrium between the contraction and relaxation of the tissues, and a balance of function between stimulation and sedation. The famous set of axes formed by these ideas is familiar to most students of herbal medicine (Fig. 7.1). The line of the horizontal axis, with a contracted state at one extreme and a relaxed state at the other, represents the muscle fibres supplying the particular organ. The vertical axis has at its north end the stimulated state, and at its southern extreme the sedated state. The point of intersection of the two lines represents the point of equilibrium for the organism, and it is the aim of the practitioner to restore that state of balance when disease disturbs it. If, for example, the nervous system deviates from its normal point of equilibrium, to become what the physiomedicalists would describe as 'over-contracted', then the individual will show symptoms such as anxiety or agitation. If there is an 'over-relaxed' state, then there will be reduced response to stimuli. In the case of the latter, the practitioner prescribes herbs that are stimulatory to the nervous system. Thurston classified the herbs according to where they acted on this set of axes. A full classification of herbs based on this can be found in Priest and Priest (1982). Much of this information is still relevant today, and the actions are fully backed up by biochemical analyses of the herbs.

The interplay of herbs with homeostasis is the central theme of western herbal medicine. Herbs are used to help restore a natural balance, their actions being carefully considered against the background of the functional disorder as a treatment regime is planned. Because the composition of a tincture can be varied so easily, regular alterations can be made, reflecting the changes that are occurring in the body as it readjusts. Such a highly flexible approach is in stark contrast to the repeated relatively high doses of a single compound when an allopathic drug is prescribed. Such a substance will exert precisely the same effect at each dose. Since it is not really possible to know precisely when the equilibrium has been re-established, several of the later doses of a drug may not really be required, and indeed may start to have a deleterious effect on what has now become a 'normal' physiology. Although it is similarly very

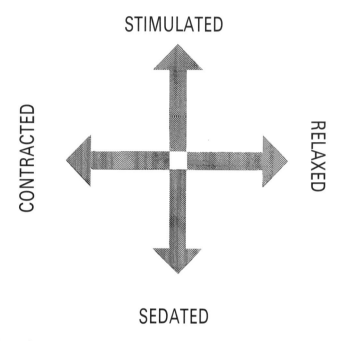

STIMULATED

CONTRACTED

RELAXED

SEDATED

Figure 7.1. The physiomedical axes.

difficult when administering herbal medicine to be certain when the end point has been reached, the much lower concentration of individual compounds will exert a less dramatic effect.

References

Beach, W. (1859). *The Reformed Practice of Medicine*. Birmingham.

Cook, W.H. (1879). *The Science and Practice of Medicine*. William Morrow.

Korr, I. M. (1991). Osteopathic research: the needed paradigm shift. *J. Am. Osteopath. Ass.*, **91(2)**, 156–68.

Priest, A. W. and Priest, L. R. (1982). *Herbal Medication: A Clinical and Dispensary Handbook*. The Stanhope Press.

Thurston, J. M. (1900). *Philosophy of Physiomedicalism*. Indiana.

Voltaire, in Strauss, M. B. (1968). *Familiar Medical Quotations*, p. 394. Little Brown and Co.

Watson, J. K. (1991). The philosophical basis of traditional Chinese medicine and the implications for its clinical evaluation. *J. Chin. Med.*, **36**, 14–17.

8

Research

The mysterious world of the paradigm

Extensive discourses on paradigms make the automatic assumption that researchers/practitioners are familiar with the word – yet finding a definition poses the first problem. A paradigm is best thought of as an abstract conceptual model that purports to define how scientific theory and methodologies are viewed. It is a relatively new term within the field of science, having been adopted by Kuhn in 1962. Recently, however, we have become preoccupied with it to such an extent that no discussion on complementary medicine research is considered complete without it. Masterman (1995) points out that it has been used in 21 different ways. If it can be used in so many different senses, how useful is it in a research context?

It is postulated that the paradigms of conventional (orthodox) medicine and complementary medicine are separate and do not overlap. The induction follows that research methodologies applied to one discipline cannot be applied to the other. This sweeping generalization cannot universally be applied because some areas of complementary medicine, for example herbal medicine, have approaches that are much 'closer' to the orthodox approach than others. Thus, the design of research programmes within these areas should not pose insurmountable problems.

Much has been written about the concept of the paradigm, and research in complementary medicine has largely become preoccupied with such considerations. This move of emphasis away from practical aspects has done little to promote the front-line research that is so desperately needed. Philosophers have adopted the concept of the paradigm and nurtured it as a central theme of research in complementary medicine. This has led to a great deal of introverted discussion, impeding clinically-based research that would actually benefit patients. Because it is so vague, we would be at no obvious disadvantage without the paradigm.

The general public demonstrates a powerful interest in many areas of complementary medicine, the most popular being osteopathy, homoeopathy, herbal medicine and acupuncture. This is partly due to dissatisfaction with certain aspects of orthodox medicine, and partly due to a desire to decrease dependency on 'drugs', seeking a more 'natural' alternative. The growing popularity of such therapies is totally unaffected by philosophical debate on paradigms within academia. Therefore, a more useful activity would be to ask the question 'how may communication between doctors and medical herbalists be improved?' rather than dwelling on descriptions of theoretical differences between them. We cannot accept that the spheres of orthodox medicine and herbal medicine are completely separate and do not overlap. In fact, there are GPs who hold qualifications in both disciplines. One wonders which paradigm they are working in.

Lack of communication

Improvement in communication will allow greater understanding of herbal medicine, and a full appreciation of its benefits will follow. This applies to any branch of complementary medicine. The abstract discussions on philosophical matters which seem to dominate exploration of complementary medicine research often appear misplaced when so many people are still unaware of what certain branches of complementary medicine actually are. All patients at Wapping Health Centre who consult the medical herbalist are asked about herbal medicine and, not surprisingly, the great majority of them are unaware of what the treatment involves. Some tend to think that they are likely to have to make up their own medicines from dried herbs, and others assume they are taking homoeopathic preparations. It is the duty of all those who practise complementary medicine to communicate precisely what they practise.

Sadly, knowledge of European herbal medicine tends to be kept 'in house', as illustrated by the range of books available. Most of these fall into one of two categories: either detailed herbals for the practitioner, or herbals for 'Mr and Mrs Average', who may want to extend their knowledge of garden herbs. There are very few which present a scientific approach and, consequently, people continue to confuse Chinese herbalism with European herbal medicine and homoeopathy. Because so few texts seek to inform the medical profession, they also add to the confusion. Many patients ask their GPs about herbal medicine, and often receive very inaccurate information. Thus the muddle is propagated. Interestingly, a survey of articles in the popular press concerning herbal medicine reveals that they rarely make any attempt to distinguish between the different areas. Many articles are specifically designed to act as 'scare stories', warning their readers about the 'dangers' of liver damage and related issues, and contain the same, recycled, out-of-date material.

What *is* research in herbal medicine?

Research within the branch of complementary medicine defined as herbal medicine is not the same as research into plant-derived isolates, since these are individual compounds. There is great activity within the latter area because drug companies are very keen to identify substances that might form the basis of a new drug, especially with reference to antiviral agents that might be anti-HIV in action. Regular reports appear in the media concerning the race to identify, extract, and investigate substances derived from rare species found in certain habitats. The best-known examples are plants from the fast disappearing rainforest ecosystems. The indigenous human populations possess a vast oral tradition concerning local herbal medicine, and many researchers are attempting to make a written record of this before the habitats are removed and lost forever during deforestation schemes. Such research is, however, out of context as far as practitioners of herbal medicine are concerned, since it deals with individual chemical substances rather than the whole-plant extracts – which is the way in which the local population would use them.

Such projects are regularly reported in the news, and this gives the overall impression that there is a lot of research going on in 'herbal medicine'. However, this is not the case. Research into the physiological effects of whole-plant extracts as prescribed by medical herbalists is virtually non-existent.

There have been very few studies that acknowledge this difference in approach. However, Farnsworth *et al.* (1985) presented a comprehensive study of the role of medicinal plants in primary health care. A comparison was made between the use of medicinal species in the traditional context, and the known pharmacological action of 119 different isolates. It was found that 74 per cent of the isolates exhibited a pharmacological effect consistent with their use within traditional medicine. In other words, when the plants were chemically analysed, they were found to contain substances that did indeed bring about the effects described by the generations of those who had used them as traditional remedies. The conclusion drawn from this study is that, since such a high percentage of plants investigated did indeed show activity directly related to historical use, it might well be profitable to invest in mass screening of potentially useful species. It is also suggested that, in poorer communities, plants could be better utilized, and even used to replace expensive imported pharmaceutical preparations.

Interestingly, this research also draws attention to the difficulty in reproducing much of the data on the physiological activity of the plant extracts. It is suggested that this may be due to the fact that much of the testing has been carried out on laboratory animals that are malnourished, and thus will respond differently to the active principles. Also, it must be remembered that the plant extracts will naturally show genetic variation, and will not therefore contain exactly the same amounts of the various chemical constituents. Differences in edaphic factors and climate will introduce further variables, and the results thus become very difficult to interpret.

Research: the way forward

The main barrier to carrying out 'acceptable' research is lack of access to large numbers of patients, which would allow statistically valid data to be presented. Most studies on the effects of individual herbs have been carried out on relatively small samples of patients, virtually all of whom have been treated privately or at a centre for complementary medicine. To date, there have been no large-scale trials of western herbal medicine within the National Health Service, since herbal medicine has not yet been fully accepted into the NHS. The situation at Wapping Health Centre, where a large population of patients have unlimited access to herbal medicine, is unusual, and offers better prospects for research.

Although a somewhat uneasy subject within herbal medicine circles, it has to be admitted that medical herbalists have only relatively recently (within the last 20 years) been trained in research methodology, and are thus able to organize clinical trials. That is not to say that the training of previous generations of herbalists is inferior in any way; it simply had a different emphasis. This has to be an important factor in considering how research in herbal medicine has developed and is currently evolving. Now that Bachelor of Science courses in herbal medicine have been established, students have full access to university facilities and future links with medical schools could well be developed, opening up new horizons. But how do we encourage such links?

Those who see herbal medicine as a genuinely complementary science, rather than an 'alternative' one, are earnestly striving to prove how comfortably it lies alongside mainstream treatment.

Unfortunately, this is not the position of all herbalists. Those who live in the past and stubbornly ignore the latest scientific developments, such as the wealth of data available from biochemical analyses, are simply slowing down the rate of acceptance of herbal medicine. Most importantly, in so doing they effectively decrease its availability to patients who would greatly benefit from it. It should be the aim of all those professionals who practise herbal medicine to increase its acceptability within medical circles, thus increasing its availability to patients. Those who insist that they cannot 'mix with orthodoxy', as if their herbal science can be poisoned by the allopathic approach, are gravely mistaken. Rather, the allopathic approach has a lot to learn from our more holistic one, and medical herbalists have a lot to gain from being incorporated into a health practice setting. The Wapping Health Centre experience clearly demonstrates this.

The practice of herbal medicine does not have to be compromised in any way, but it must move with the times, as it always has done, abandoning previous beliefs for those which allow its most effective use. Participation in clinical trials is a natural progression, and medical herbalists should be keen to participate in such areas of research, which will help to demonstrate efficacy. The closeted concept amongst certain herbalists that 'we know it works, and that is sufficient' is a very negative one. To deliberately ignore the knowledge gained from advances in analytical methods is short sighted, and can only attract the opinion from within mainstream medicine that herbalists continue to be 'unscientific' in their approach. This is reminiscent of the situation in the last century, when there was a deep rift between mainstream practitioners and herbalists, who were deemed to be somewhat simplistic in their approach to treatment.

The historical use of herbs is very important, but we must recognize that it will never be accepted by medical researchers as valid proof of action and efficacy. What we should be concerned with is pointing out that traditional uses of herbs can be substantiated by modern analyses of their chemical constituents. The ancient common names of plants are remarkably accurate reflections of their principle action; for example staunchwort (*Achillea millefolium*) has a marked haemostatic action.

Back to basics

Research in any branch of science involves asking a question or testing a hypothesis. This is a universal starting point. The actual methodology employed obviously depends on the nature of the investigation. Within herbal medicine there is enormous scope for research, due to the range of the *materia medica* and its overall broad similarity in approach to that of mainstream medicine. The ground rules for testing the effects of drugs or intervention procedures are laid down within orthodox medicine in that clinical trials have a rigid framework that must be adhered to. By applying the same rules to herbal medicine, valid results can be obtained.

Research : the current situation

The design of research methodologies for herbal medicine is not without its difficulties. Outwardly it would seem that, since the tinctures used in western herbal medicine are taken by mouth, it should be relatively straightforward to investigate the efficacy of a given plant tincture in a similar manner to that applied to any drug. However, as will be seen, this is not the case.

Firstly, very few treatments in herbal medicine involve the prescription of just one herb (see Chapter 5). Even when this is the case, because we are always dealing with an extract of a whole plant, it effectively involves the administration of several hundred different substances – even though in practice only a very small percentage are at therapeutic levels. Although we are aware what these substances are, as well as their main actions, it would be very difficult to relate the chemical composition of the tincture to all the observed physiological effects. Orthodoxy is highly suspicious of the application of material containing so many different substances. Dr D. G. Davey, a former Research Director of ICI, once commented: 'If a cabbage was subjected to spectroscopic analysis and presented to the Committee on the Safety of Medicines, it would be rejected outright' (Davey, 1978). However, he stressed that drugs are some of the 'purest' substances that we have. The pharmaceutical industry has left behind all those plant species that were the source of so many medicines, and is now concentrating on manufacturing synthetic versions of the naturally produced molecules – but what price purity? Side effects are hardly rare events within mainstream medicine, and we would do well to recall Sir Derrick Dunlop's adage: 'Show me a medicine without adverse effects and I will show you a useless medicine'.

Under normal circumstances, since the prescription consists of about four to six different herbs, we are delivering a highly complex medicine. This greatly magnifies the problem. Furthermore, at the keystone of herbal medicine is the belief that it is the combination of these substances that brings about a sustained therapeutic effect; the observed effect is more than the sum of the parts. As may be appreciated, it is this highly variable approach to prescription that makes western herbal medicine appear difficult to analyse.

Medical herbalists are in a difficult position; their treatments need to be subjected to 'scientific' testing if herbal medicine is to gain credibility within scientific circles. On the other hand, the accepted means of testing the efficacy of treatments, namely the clinical trial, is not ideally suited to herbal medicine. Not only might such a trial give very misleading results, but it also cannot fit a therapy that has at its heart an individually tailored treatment for each patient. To ask herbal medicine to submit to this means of evaluation is not necessarily the way forward. Currently, however, the clinical trial is the only test given general credibility within contemporary circles, and it is used to fulfil legislative criteria for medicines. Despite scattered historical references to comparative studies, the true clinical trial involving, in addition to the comparative aspect, both randomization and blind assessment components, is a relatively modern phenomenon. The first mention of a trial with both randomization of patients and provision for the double-blind administration of a drug was that concerning the use of sanocrysin in the treatment of pulmonary tuberculosis in 1931 (Burns Amberson *et al.*, 1931). It was first described in full in 1934 (Therapeutic Trials Committee of the Medical Research Council). The clinical trial has evolved to become an active area of research within its own right – to such an extent that, in 1979, a Society for Clinical Research was set up in the United States. Even so, the clinical trial as a means of testing is not without its critics. It is regularly questioned within mainstream medicine, especially with respect to the ethical aspects of the placebo.

Plant placebos

Given that western herbal medicines are mainly in the form of tinctures, consideration needs to be given to the question of placebos. What type of placebo could be given within the context of a clinical trial? How similar to the actual tincture would the placebo tincture have to be in order to be acceptable? To answer these questions, several factors must be considered. Firstly, to what extent are the patients familiar with herbal medicines (and their extremely acquired tastes)? Secondly, to what extent do the patients themselves interact? If patients as a group discuss their medication, then the placebo must be as close to the actual medicine as possible in terms of taste, colour, odour, etc. Such problems do not arise when standard drug trials are carried out, since medications are usually solids given in the form of tablets or capsules. Unpleasant tasting material can be encapsulated, and differences in, for example, colour between the drug and the placebo can likewise be disguised by utilization of a capsule. This is not possible with a liquid.

The individual approach is an integral part of herbal medicine. Perhaps it should become more of a focus in clinical research, and it has been suggested that there should be more randomized controlled trials in individual patients (*Drug and Therapeutics Bulletin*, May 1998). The conclusion is that the results of large-scale trials may not help in deciding the treatment for an individual patient, which is, of course, the main criticism voiced by many practitioners of complementary medicine. A 'single patient trial' involves assessing a treatment against a second treatment or a placebo, and it is suggested that the two treatments (A and B) could be randomized (for example, AAABBABAAB, etc.). This regime appears to allow a more rigorous assessment of a treatment, particularly when dealing with a chronic or recurrent condition that responds rapidly to treatment. The one obvious disadvantage is that it is a very time-consuming approach; also, the same statistical tests as those applied to large-scale trials may not be applicable. Thus it has to be concluded that, although it is refreshing to see a trial being carried out at the individual patient level, this is unlikely to become the standard means of testing, and will only be useful in a limited number of clinical situations. However, the single patient trial could be considered acceptable as a means of testing those treatments such as herbal medicine that are more suited to a study involving a single patient. If such a means of research was adopted, the results would not only be considered scientifically valid, but would be meaningful in that they relate to herbal medicine as it is actually practised – that is, on an individual level. Such results would be useful in a clinical context, as future management plans could be directly related to previous experience. This proposed change of emphasis is reminiscent of a case study approach, which is the main way of presenting clinical data within complementary medicine.

There has always been doubt regarding the usefulness of clinical trials within herbal medicine. By necessity, clinical trials are procedures designed to analyse the efficacy of a particular treatment in statistical terms. As such, they will never be able to analyse this branch of complementary medicine, where the very definition of the therapy involves an individual approach. Offering an identical treatment to a large batch of patients would never occur in practice, so an artificial situation is immediately set up. It could be argued that the clinical trial is always an artificial event; however, it is fair to say that within mainstream medicine large numbers of patients **do** routinely receive the same treatment. This is never the case in herbal medicine.

How widespread and how useful are the results of clinical trials within orthodox medicine? A survey of published research over a period of 10 years revealed that only approximately one in six studies were randomized controlled trials, and almost 50 per cent were descriptive observational studies of treatment. Of those that were actual experiments, one-third lacked a control and another one-third utilized non-random controls. Thus, the use of the classical randomized controlled trial is not as widespread as might be thought. This is because its limitations are well recognized, and not all treatments can be subjected to such analysis – for example, in surgery the double-blind aspect has no meaning. Furthermore, rigid exclusion criteria have to be applied to ensure homogeneity, which therefore results in a set of cases that are unrepresentative of the condition in general (Fletcher and Fletcher, 1979).

As can be seen, clinical trials are not without their problems, and they cannot be applied universally within orthodox medicine. So why should they be the main means by which complementary therapies such as herbal medicine should be tested? If 50 per cent of published research within mainstream medicine consists of purely descriptive work, then the case history studies that characterize many areas of complementary medicine should be equally acceptable. Research in complementary medicine will continue to lag behind mainstream medical research if it does not manage to muster sufficient activation energy. Lack of such energy cannot, however, be blamed entirely for lack of progress; practitioners have not always had access to large numbers of patients. However, now that access is available, we should be willing to enter an exponential phase of development rather than concentrate on theoretical debates that lead nowhere.

Research update

At the time of going to press (January 1999), some exciting research developments are under way. A clinical investigation of the use of *Ulmus fulva* (slippery elm) is planned by both authors and the Special Immunity Service and Pharmacy Departments at St. Bartholomew's Hospital in London. Gastrointestinal symptoms are a common feature of chronic fatigue syndrome (CFS), often with a very variable aetiology and presentation. Treatment using a single allopathic medication is therefore problematic, since this can only deal with one symptom. This study utilizes a pharmaceutically prepared tablet of the inner cortex (bark) of *Ulmus fulva* (slippery elm) and, because it is not an isolate, Ulmus is able to address a range of symptoms. Since the components of Ulmus are mainly high molecular weight polysaccharides, it is largely unabsorbed from the gastrointestinal tract. It has been routinely prescribed to patients at Wapping Health Centre by both researchers for several years. There are no recorded side effects, and no known interactions with allopathic drugs. It is hoped to provide a safe and effective agent for the treatment of bloating, abdominal pain and constipation.

The aim of the study is to provide statistically significant, verified evidence as to the efficacy of this safe herbal medication for the treatment and relief of symptoms of gastrointestinal disturbance in patients with CFS. Approximately 50 patients are to be recruited at the clinic, where the trial will be advertised by leaflet and doctor advocacy. Patients will be supplied with a symptom diary for the daily recording of the severity of three symptoms – abdominal pain, bloating, and bowel habit – on a Lickert (visual analogue) scale.

At the follow-up appointment, the patient's symptomatology will be reviewed and the diary examined. The patient will then be given medication from the hospital pharmacy at the clinic, which will also administer the medication and its randomization. Patient, researcher and pharmacist will all be blind to the intervention given, and the medication will be either *Ulmus fulva* tablets 200 mg or placebo. Further appointments will be made at approximately 2-weekly intervals, until the patient has attended five times in total. Medication and recording of symptoms will continue throughout this period.

Individual medicines at the molecular level

Ironically, orthodoxy has at last recognized on its own terms that the prescription of drugs must be tailored more to the individual patient. Pharmaceutical companies are well aware that prescribing efficacy would be improved if the genetic differences of the individual could be taken into consideration. This is the concern of a whole new science – pharmacogenomics. Not only does it aim to predict which drug is most suitable for a given genome, but it also attempts to identify those individuals that are likely to have a serious adverse reaction. At present, much prescribing (for example, of antidepressants) is little more than trial and error. When one drug such as fluoxetine does not work, the patient is given another to try.

This delays successful treatment, and possibly introduces more undesirable side effects.

Drug companies are excited by the prospects; such an individual approach is expected to increase the number of medicines reaching the market place. A particular drug will be aimed at one section of the population. This is a clear example of profit-led development.

The whole development of an individual-based prescription serves to acknowledge that drugs do not have a universal action. In 1994, adverse drug reactions accounted for over 100 000 deaths in the United States (Schmidt, 1998). The shift of reliance on clinical trial data to examination of individual genome data represents a complete change of emphasis, and companies such as Glaxo Wellcome have begun to collect DNA samples from clinical trial participants. We are already aware of many examples where genetics directly affect drug response – for example, a drug used to treat high levels of cholesterol (pravastatin) will not work if the recipient has a common gene variant for cholesterol transfer protein.

The treatment of a patient has 'progressed' from Hippocrates' holistic approach, where the whole person is considered, through a series of historical stages centred on different grades of organization. This shift from focusing on organ systems, then organs, tissues, cells, and organelles, occurred as concurrent advances in microscopy and analytical techniques proceeded.

This reductionism finds its ultimate expression in the new science of pharmacogenomics, where the whole person is represented by a sequence of DNA. The total response to a drug cannot be detected by merely examining a length of DNA, although important adverse reactions related to specific biochemical abnormalities can be identified – this is one of the few positive aspects of the development. Many factors contribute to the final response shown by the patient: age, sex, health status and potential drug interactions will all play a role.

A focus on well-researched herbs

It is not the aim of this handbook to provide details of the therapeutic actions of all the herbs used in western herbal medicine; there are a large number of books devoted to this aspect. However, since those working in general practice will undoubtedly come across several herbal medicines, particularly those purchased over-the-counter, a brief consideration of two well-known species that have been fully investigated is presented here. Finally, there is a consideration of cannabis, which has recently received much media attention.

St. John's wort (*Hypericum perforatum*)

This herb has received much attention in Europe. In Germany in 1993, general practitioners wrote 2.7 million prescriptions for it. In the United States, it is described as 'nature's Prozac'. Numerous clinical studies have confirmed that it is as effective as antidepressants in the treatment of mild depression. A large study carried out in Germany in 1994 compared the effects of Hypericum with imipramine on a group of 135 patients with depression (Vorbach *et al.*, 1994). Of the group receiving Hypericum, 75 per cent were rated as having 'greatly improved' or 'much improved', compared with 60 per cent of those on imipramine. Several studies comparing Hypericum to other commonly prescribed antidepressants have shown similar results. In 1996, Linde *et al.* re-examined all the data available for Hypericum and presented a meta-analysis. They concluded that the scores on the Hamilton Depression Scale were better for patients receiving Hypericum than those produced by patients on standard antidepressants. They also stated that: 'clinical trials suggest that Hypericum might become an important tool for the management of depressive disorders, especially in primary healthcare settings'. This is exciting recognition indeed for a herbal medicine; however, overall, orthodoxy is guarded in its praise and prefers to describe it as 'equally effective as standard medication' (Hubner *et al.*, 1994).

Hypericum has virtually no side effects, and for this reason it is becoming the 'drug' of choice in cases of anxiety, insomnia and premenstrual syndrome. It is a fact that most of those diagnosed with 'depression' in general practice are only mildly depressed, and would therefore benefit from a herbal-based treatment such as Hypericum. It is thus accepted as a safe option for the majority of people with depression (Harrer and Schulz, 1994). It is also effective for those with seasonal affective disorder (SAD) (Martinez *et al.*, 1994). However, many patients are still being prescribed Prozac, which is a toxic compound with a host of undesirable side effects. In a recent study that monitored drug side effects, 3250 patients received Hypericum and only 2.4 per cent reported side effects (Woelk *et al.*, 1994). This figure is about one-tenth of that reported for allopathic antidepressants. Even where side effects are reported, they are significantly milder than those reported with the standard antidepressant drugs used as comparisons (Vorbach, 1994; Witte *et al.*, 1995). Since Hypericum has very few side effects, it is ideal for the elderly or for those who have shown a previous sensitivity to conventional drugs (Ernst, 1995).

Hypericum is a whole-plant extract, comprising a large number of different chemical substances, and it therefore has other effects apart from the antidepressant action. It is known to have a positive effect on the immune system, as well as direct antiviral and antibacterial activity (Lavie *et al.*, 1995a). The antibiotic substances novoimanine and hyperforin have been identified (Avenirova, 1977), and a whole plant extract has been found to be effective against tuberculosis (Guseinova *et al.*, 1992). Interestingly, this action against tuberculosis had been identified by Culpepper in his herbal.

Research has demonstrated that hypericin isolated from Hypericum is active against a wide range of viruses, including herpes and hepatitis C. Activity against HIV has also been reported (Meruelo *et al.*, 1988). It has been demonstrated that hypericin acts in two different ways; it not only inactivates the virus, but also protects cell membranes from attack by viruses (Lavie *et al.*, 1995b). There is no synthetic antiviral agent capable of this dual action. Researchers at the New York Medical Center have found hypericin to be such an exciting new compound that they have applied to take out a patent. (Although the substance itself cannot be patented, its use as a specific antiviral treatment can.) The same team has successfully added hypericin to blood in order to protect against the spread of certain viruses during transfusions (Lavie *et al.*, 1995a). This is considered an inexpensive way of reducing the risk of post-transfusion infection.

During depression the immune system produces abnormally high levels of interleukins, which interfere with normal immune responses, often resulting in the patient becoming more susceptible to infections (Maes *et al.*, 1993). Thus it is often observed that those with depression have an increased incidence of conditions such as cystitis, influenza, etc. (Herbert and Cohen, 1993).

Numerous other beneficial effects of Hypericum have been studied. Relief from headache, anxiety and fatigue were recorded in a study carried out by Hubner *et al.* (1994). Hypericum has been found to be effective in the treatment of chronic insomnia. Unlike other agents it is not a sedative, but it increases the brain's natural sleep-enhancing mechanism. However, it takes approximately one week to take effect, so it is of less use where an immediate effect is required (Sommer and Harrer, 1994).

Slow on the uptake?

If Hypericum is such a useful plant with so many different uses, then why isn't it prescribed more frequently? As previously mentioned, it has gained great popularity in Germany, but elsewhere it remains mainly the domain of the medical herbalist rather than the mainstream practitioner. Although it is widely available in health food shops in Great Britain, the dried form in which it most commonly occurs does not necessarily show the greatest activity. To benefit fully, the patient needs to be accurately informed as to its best indications and dosages, as well as the best pharmaceutical preparations.

As information regarding the efficacy of herbs such as Hypericum becomes accessible to patients, they will begin to request them. Already the demand for herbal medicine is showing a steady increase. Long-standing prejudice regarding herbal medicine is still a big factor preventing access for many patients; however, this can never be as serious as the immense political influence exerted by the drug companies, which is an ever-present restraint on the acceptance of herbal medicines. The world-wide market for antidepressants alone is estimated to be worth six billion dollars. Marketing a new drug is an extremely expensive process, due to the very strict system of clinical trials and legislature designed to protect the general public from dangerous untested drugs. Having invested huge sums in launching a new synthetic drug, the drug companies must be able to patent their new products in order to ensure a monopoly on them. This allows them to maintain high charges, and ensures that large profits provide an excellent return on their investment. Unfortunately, the success of a plant such as Hypericum is of no interest whatsoever – except, of course, to the last link in the chain, the patient. Herbs cannot be patented because anyone can grow and market them. Since most research on potentially useful medicines is funded by drug companies, any that have no future as patentable items are deliberately ignored.

One might imagine that this is of no consequence to the doctors who actually prescribe the medicines and make contact with the patients requiring them. However, the information they receive about the appropriate allopathic medicines comes from the drug companies. This may either occur directly by advertising, or indirectly by the sponsoring of research programmes designed to investigate the clinical uses of a newly launched drug. Specialists in medicine may well be partially funded by grants from drug companies, which can only colour their advice to colleagues in general practice.

Inbred prejudice?

The lack of use of herbs within mainstream medicine cannot wholly be blamed on the pharmaceutical industry. The fact is that many general practitioners are prejudiced against the use of herbs as medicines. There are good reasons for this; doctors are provided with regular articles on the 'dangers' of herbal medicines (see Chapter 6), and others warning of the possible interactions between standard medicines and herbal medicines. Not unreasonably, they are unwilling to take the chance of prescribing something when they do not fully understand its action. Herbal medicine does not feature in detail in any undergraduate course in medicine. However, in an attempt to inform trainee general practitioners about complementary medicine, certain authorities (e.g. the East London and the City Health Authority) now provide seminars, with specialists in each of the different disciplines explaining the basis of their particular therapy. As far as the classical medical school curriculum is concerned, the only reference to herbal medicine is usually the fact that many of today's medicines (such as morphine, aspirin and digoxin) were originally extracted from plants. It is also pointed out that the process of extraction makes the isolated product far superior to the original form in which it occurs in the plant. Having removed all the other 'useless' substances, the activity of the isolate is far easier to predict and thus 'safer'. This 'fact' is doggedly adhered to without question, regardless of what the use of herbal medicine might otherwise indicate. Single substances are the rule, and this is not to be questioned – certainly not by herbalists. Interestingly, however, this rule may be undergoing modification. In the case of the research on Hypericum, it has now been recommended by researchers within orthodox medicine that it is better to take an extract of the whole plant, rather than a standardized extract of hypericin, as the former has a number of substances that are antidepressant in action (Harrer and Schulz, 1994). Apparently, researchers have not been able to identify a single substance that would account for all the observed therapeutic effects. They have finally 'discovered' what herbalists have known and practised for centuries; the observed action of a herb is never due to a single chemical substance. This is the embodiment of the practice of western herbal medicine.

An improvement on nature?

Having acknowledged that Hypericum is indeed a very useful plant, what could be the future role of the drug companies, given that they must accept that the whole plant can never be patented? At least one research team is busy considering how to 'develop' its pharmaceutical potential. Yip *et al.* (1996) described a modification of the hypericin molecule, yielding potential antiviral effects. If this can indeed be marketed, since the molecule is no longer identical to that occurring in nature, then it may legally form the basis of a new antidepressant drug, as well as millions of dollars of new profit. The fact that the public does not need it is irrelevant; the companies are seeking the profit it is capable of attracting.

Echinacea

This is a very well-known medicinal herb and, like Hypericum, it is widely available as an over-the-counter medicine. Two main species are involved: *Echinacea angustifolia* and *Echinacea purpurea*. Usually the roots are used, although some medicines are prepared from the leaves or, less commonly, the whole plant. It is now extensively cultivated in Europe, although it originated in the North American prairies. The historical use of this genus to treat infections and a variety of skin complaints is validated by biochemical analyses. The main constituents include caffeic acid derivatives, such as echinoside, cichoric acid and cynarin, which have all been shown to exhibit antibacterial and antiviral activity (Houghton, 1994). Other compounds present include the lipophilic polyacetylenes, alkamides, and volatile oil components, including sesquiterpenes. It has been found that the polysaccharides reduce inflammation, and the alkamides inhibit lipoxygenase. Two main immunostimulatory polysaccharides have been identified (PSI and PSII). The first (a 4-O-methyl glucuronoarabinoxylan) is built up of glucuronic acid together with arabinose and xylose, and the second (an acidicarabinorhamnogalactan) comprises rhamnose, arabinose and galactose (Bauer and Wagner, 1991). The alkylamides are an interesting group of lesser-known secondary plant metabolites, and are the group responsible for bringing about the tingling sensation on the tongue when Echinacea is taken as a liquid preparation. They are formed from the combination of a carboxylic acid and an amine; it is suggested that the bond uniting these two molecules is hydrolysed during digestion, and that it is the carboxylic acid that is pharmacologically active (Bauer and Wagner, 1991). Echinacea is promoted as being an immune system stimulant; its main action appears to be via the promotion of phagocytosis, and activation of T and B lymphocytes. It is less well known as a herb used in topical treatments, although trials using an ointment containing an extract of Echinacea show promising results for the treatment of burns, which is one of its traditional uses. Studies have shown no adverse effects or poisoning, even at very high doses (Houghton, 1994).

The cannabis controversy

The media, the public and the medical profession are taking a close look at this medicinal herb, the therapeutic effects of which were first recorded more than 150 years ago (O'Shaughnessy, 1842). Early observations on its anticonvulsant and muscle relaxant properties led to it being widely prescribed for various conditions. Consequently, cannabis is found in many nineteenth and early twentieth century publications; its inclusion is not just restricted to herbals such as *The New Family Herbal and Botanic Physician* (Robinson, 1872). It is listed in inexpensive medical dictionaries such as *Beeton's Shilling Medical Dictionary*, found in virtually every household around the time of the First World War. It also appears in the *British Pharmacopoeia* up until the mid-1940s.

It has been illegal to prescribe cannabis in the UK since the introduction of the 1971 Misuse of Drugs Act, and this legal status has effectively prevented active research into its undoubted properties. Although recent media coverage has highlighted its use in relieving several of the symptoms associated with multiple sclerosis (MS), including reduction of muscle spasm and tremor (Wills, 1995), it has many other applications (Petro and Ellenberger, 1981). Research has been carried out into its possible use in treating motor tics in Tourette's syndrome and torsion dystonia (Sadyk *et al.*, 1988), and in Huntington's chorea (Moss *et al.*, 1989). For those with epilepsy who fail to respond to conventional drugs, it may act as an efficient anticonvulsant (Consroe *et al.*, 1975). Since cannabis causes bronchodilation, work has been done on testing cannabinoids as potential anti-asthma drugs (Tashkin *et al.*, 1975). It has even shown promise as an antibacterial substance (Radosevic *et al.*, 1962). Although there are reported insignificant side effects, there have been no recorded deaths from cannabis use (Gray, 1995).

Serious medical research into its potential as a most useful herbal medicine is overshadowed by debates regarding whether a change in its legal status should be implemented. Meanwhile, drug companies are focusing their efforts, as usual, in preparing for clinical use of 'pure' isolates of cannabinoids, over 60 of which have been identified (Wills, 1995). Commercially, the most important is Δ-9-tetrahydrocannabinol (THC). In the UK, the synthetic cannabinoid nabilone is licensed for use as an anti-emetic for those undergoing chemotherapy. In the USA, an oral form of THC is used as an appetite stimulant in AIDS patients, as well as an anti-emetic. Commercial activities centred on isolated compounds bypass the legal status of the whole herb, which accordingly becomes irrelevant.

Cannabis has been described as a 'pharmacologically dirty drug, containing many active substances with multiple effects and unknown modes of action. The wealth of ingredients presents both problems and opportunities' (Gray, 1995). Alas, the only opportunities that are recognized are those for the pharmaceutical industry to develop new patented drugs, rather than the far-reaching clinical opportunities provided by administering the whole plant. The actual 'problems' referred to appear to be that the whole plant can never be patented to provide a further source of profit; therefore the patient will never fully benefit.

References

Avenirova, E. L. (1977). Effect of novoimanine on the cellular permeability indices of staphylococci. *Antibiotiki*, **7**, 630–34.

Bauer, R. and Wagner, H. (1991). Echinacea species as potential immunstimulatory drugs. In *Economic and Medicinal Plant Research*, Vol. 5, pp. 253–322. Academic Press.

Beeton's Medical Dictionary: A Safe Guide for Every Family (early 1900s; undated). Ward Lock.

Burns Amberson, J., McMahon, B. T. and Pinner, M. (1931). A clinical trial of sanocrysin in pulmonary tuberculosis. *Amer. Rev. Tuberculosis*, **24**, 401–35.

Consroe, P., Wood, G. C. and Buchsbaum, H. (1975). Anticonvulsive nature of marihuana smoking. *JAMA*, **234**, 306–7.

Davey, D. (1978). In *Alternative Medicine* (R. Eagle, ed.). Futura Publications.

Drug and Therapeutics Bulletin (1998). Randomized controlled trials in single patients. *DTB*, **36(5)**.

Ernst, E. (1995). St. John's wort, an antidepressant: a systematic criteria-based review. *Phytomedicine*, **2(1)**, 67–71.

Farnsworth, N. R., Akerle, O., Bingel, A. S. *et al.* (1985). Medicinal plants in therapy. *Bull. WHO*, **63(6)**, 965–81.

Fletcher, R. H. and Fletcher, S. W. (1979). Clinical research in general medical journals. *N. Engl. J. Med.*, **301**, 180–83.

Gray, C. (1995). Cannabis – the therapeutic potential. *Pharm. J.*, **254**, 771–3.

Guseinova, V. E. *et al.* (1992). Examining the antimicrobial properties of medicinal plant species. *Farmatsiya*, **41(4)**, 21–4.

Harrer, G. and Schulz, V. (1994). Clinical investigation of the antidepressant effectiveness of hypericum. *J. Geriatr. Psych. Neur.*, **7**(Suppl. 1), S6–8.

Herbert, T. B. and Cohen, S. (1994). Depression and immunity: a meta-analytic review. *Psych. Bull.*, **1133**, 472–86.

Houghton, P. (1994). Echinacea. *Pharm. J.*, **253**, 342–3.

Hubner, W. D., Lande, S. and Podzuweit, H. (1994). Hypericum treatment of mild depressions with somatic symptoms. *J. Geriatr. Psych. Neur.*, **7**(Suppl. 1), S12–14.

Kuhn, T. S. (1962). *The Structure of Scientific Revolutions*. Chicago University Press.

Lavie, G. *et al.* (1995a). Hypericin as an inactivator of infectious viruses in blood components. *Transfusion*, **35(5)**, 392–400.

Lavie, G. *et al.* (1995b). The chemical and biological properties of hypericin – a compound with a broad spectrum of biological activities. *Med. Res. Rev.*, **15(2)**, 111–19.

Linde, K. *et al.* (1996). St. John's wort for depression – an overview and meta-analysis of randomized clinical trials. *Br. Med. J.,* **313,** 253–8.

Maes, M. *et al.* (1993). Relationships between interleukin-6 activity, acute phase proteins, and function of the hypothalamic–pituitary–adrenal axis in severe depression. *Psychiatr. Res.,* **49(1),** 11–27.

Martinez, B., Kasper, S., Ruhrmann, S. and Moller, H. J. (1994). Hypericum in the treatment of seasonal affective disorder. *J. Geriatr. Psych. Neur.,* **7**(Suppl. 1), S29–33.

Masterman, M. (1965). The nature of the paradigm. In *Criticism and the Growth of Knowledge* (I. Lakatos and A. Musgrave, eds). Cambridge University Press.

Meruelo, D., Lavie, G. and Lavie, D. (1988). Therapeutic agents with dramatic antiretroviral activity and little toxicity at effective doses: aromatic polycyclic diones hypericin and pseudohypericin. *Proc. Natl. Acad. Sci. USA,* **85(14),** 5230–34.

Moss, D. E., Manderscheeid, P. Z., Montgomery, S. P. *et al.* (1989). Nicotine and cannabinoids as adjuncts to neuroleptics in the treatment of Tourette's syndrome and other motor disorders. *Life Sci.,* **44,** 1521–5.

O'Shaughnessy, W. B. (1842). On the preparation of the Indian hemp or gunjah (*Cannabis indica*): the effects of the animal system in health, and their utility in the treatment of tetanus and other convulsive disorders. *Trans. Med. Phys. Soc. Bombay,* **8,** 421.

Petro, D. J. and Ellenberger, C. (1981). Treatment of human spasticity with D-9-THC. *J. Clin. Pharmacol.,* **21,** 413–16.

Robinson, M. (1872). *The New Family Herbal and Botanic Physician.* William Nicolson.

Rodosevic, A., Kupinic, M. and Grilic, L. (1962). Antibiotic activity of various types of cannabis resin. *Nature,* **195,** 1007–9.

Sadyk, R. and Awerbuch, G. (1998). Marijuana and Tourette's syndrome. *J. Clin. Phsychopharmacol.,* 444–5.

Schmidt, K. (1998). Just for you. *New Scientist,* 14 November.

Sommer, H. and Harrer, G. (1994). Placebo-controlled double-blind study examining the effectiveness of an hypericum preparation in the 105 mildly depressed patients. *J. Geriatr. Psych. Neur.,* **7**(Suppl. 1), S9–11.

Tashkin, D. P., Reiss, S., Shapiro, B. J. *et al.* (1975). Bronchial effects of aerosolized D-9-THC in healthy and asthmatic subjects. *Am. Rev. Resp. Dis..,* **115,** 57–65.

Vorbach, E. U., Hubner, W. D. and Arnoldt, K. H. (1994). Effectiveness and tolerance of the hypericum extract LI 160 in comparison with imipramine: randomized double-blind study with 135 patients. *J. Geriatr. Psych. Neur.,* **7**(Suppl. 1), S19–23.

Wills, S. (1995). The use of cannabis in multiple sclerosis. *Pharm. J.,* **255,** 237–8.

Witte, B. *et al.* (1995). Treatment of depressive symptoms with a high concentration Hypericum preparation. A multicenter placebo-controlled double-blind study. *Fortschritte der Medizin,* **113,** 404–8.

Woelk, H., Burkard, G. and Grunwald, J. (1994). Benefits and risks of the hypericum extract LI 160: drug monitoring study with 3250 patients. *J. Geriatr. Psych. Neur.,* **7**(Suppl. 1), S34–8.

Yip, L. *et al.* (1996). Antiviral activity of a derivative of the photosensitive compound hypericin. *Phytomedicine,* **3(2),** 185–90.

Suggested reading

Hollister, L. E. (1986). Health aspects of cannabis. *Pharmacol. Rev.*, **38**, 1–20.

Lilienfield, A. M. (1982). Ceteris Paribus: The evolution of the clinical trial. *Bull. Hist. Med.*, **56**, 1–18.

McGourty, H. (1993). How to evaluate complementary therapies: A literature review. *Liverpool Public Health Observatory Report No.13.*

Mills, S. (1986). Conflicting research needs in complementary medicine. *Compl. Med. Res.*, **1**, 40–47.

St. George, D. (1994). Towards a research and development strategy for complementary medicine. *Homoeopath*, **54**.

Zuess, J. (1997). *The Natural Prozac Program.* Three Rivers Press.

9

Conditions that respond particularly well to herbal medicine

It is not the aim of this book to provide full clinical details of treatment using herbal medicine. However, a selection of those conditions that have been found to respond particularly well to herbal medicine has been included in order to help identify the type of complaints it may be used for within general practice. It is hoped that this may encourage those involved in primary health care to consider including sessions in western herbal medicine in their practices. Since irritable bowel syndrome (IBS) is a particular interest of the herbalist at Wapping Health Centre, this condition has been considered in more detail. Table 9.1 provides a summary of the conditions seen over a period of one year.

Table 9.1. Summary of conditions seen in one year (1997–1998)

Conditions referred	Approximate percentage of total consultations
Irritable bowel syndrome (IBS)	25.8
Eczema	15.2
Depression	6.6
Acne/related skin conditions	6.3
Nutritional advice	6.3
PMT/dysmenorrhoea	5.5
Psoriasis	3.5
Menopausal complaints	3.5
Respiratory infections/sinusitis	3.1
Cystitis	3.1
Rheumatoid arthritis	2.7
Migraine	2.7
Asthma	1.6
Insomnia	1.2
Chronic fatigue syndrome (CFS)	1.2
HIV	1.2
Ulcerative colitis/Crohn's disease	0.7
Others	9.0

Recurrent urinary infection

Recurrent urinary infection is one of the most common infections encountered within general practice. It also commonly tends to recur after a course of treatment if the predisposing factors remain. There are a variety of causes for the re-infection; for example, inadequate fluid intake leads to low urine output and infrequency. With such a limited flush-out mechanism, the infection tends to persist.

Integral to the whole approach to treatment is a detailed analysis of diet, which also includes a discussion of fluid intake. In a surprisingly high number of cases the actual fluid intake is very low (well under one litre per day). It therefore becomes very important to advise the patient on how to increase fluid intake. For those who genuinely find it difficult to take in the bulk of their fluid as drinks, detailed advice is provided on foods that have a high water content. Many patients are quite happy to drink soups etc. regularly instead of pure water. For those who are well below the daily recommended level, a regime of gradually increased fluid intake is suggested. This involves advising patients to purchase small (250 ml or 500 ml) bottles of mineral water and drinking first one, then two per day. This not only provides a practical way of demonstrating just how much fluid they should be taking, but makes it far easier for them to increase their daily intake in stages.

There may also be incomplete bladder emptying, with a resultant post-micturition residue. Where the bladder outlet is obstructed (for example, in constipation, urethral stricture and prostatic hypertrophy), this becomes a reservoir of infection, which therefore persists. Other causes of recurrent infection may include reduced immune function and inappropriate use of antibiotics. The latter are very useful agents where the infection is identified and a sensitivity test has been carried out. However, there are disadvantages to their use. They have the effect of altering the species composition of the normal flora of those regions close to the region where the infection originates, for example the large intestine and distal urethra. This commonly allows resistant species to dominate over those that are sensitive to antibacterial agents, making the infection progressively more difficult to treat. Also, there is the danger of destroying those species of bacteria that are responsible for protecting the distal urethra from attack by pathogenic bowel bacteria. The kidney may also be involved; the presence of a structure such as a pyelonephritic scar can mean that there is a lingering focus of infection, virtually inaccessible to antibiotics. Infection may similarly persist where there has been chronic cystitis with severe inflammation of the bladder wall, or in the presence of a catheter.

There are a number of plants that can be employed to treat those cases where there is an active infection. The one most commonly prescribed at this health centre is *Barosma betulina* (buchu), which has a direct antibacterial action. This is mainly due to its volatile oil content (1.5–2.5 per cent), which includes pulegone, limonene, camphor, and menthone, as well as the phenolic compound diosphenol (Blommaert and Bartel, 1976). *Arctostaphylos uva-ursi* (bearberry) is another highly effective urinary antiseptic. One of its component glycosides, arbutin, is hydrolysed to release the aglycone component hydroquinone, which is antibacterial. Many other glycosides possess aglycone components that, once released from their associated sugar, will exert antiseptic properties on the kidney tubule. A study of the biochemistry of those herbs used as urinary antiseptics will reveal that they all share relatively high levels of volatile oils, resins, glycosides, saponins and tannins.

Buchu is prescribed with other herbs that act to soothe the epithelia, so plants high in mucilages are often included. Some commonly used examples include *Althaea officinalis* (mallow), *Agropyron repens* (couch grass) and *Zea mays* (cornsilks). When dealing with the urinary tract, it is a distinct advantage that the medicine is in liquid (tincture) form and is taken several times a day. Not only is it rapidly absorbed, but it is also regularly being filtered off during ultrafiltration in the kidney to act over the whole length of the nephron as well as the bladder and ureter. Following a 2–4 week course of treatment (depending on past history), the symptoms usually resolve. The use of herbal medicine is especially appropriate where repeated re-infection has become virtually unavoidable; for instance, where it follows sexual intercourse. In this case it is possible to work out a regime where a tincture can be given as a form of prophylaxis, which avoids the necessity of the regular use of antibiotics.

To increase the effect of the urinary antiseptic herbs, it is often recommended that they are taken as teas. This augments the total fluid intake, as well as increasing the exposure of the urinary system to the active principles. However, it depends on the individual patient's circumstances. For a person in full-time employment, it is not realistic to advise taking five to six cups a day when the tea has to be specially prepared from a mixture of dried herbs. Here, the tincture is more appropriate. However, where the patient is at home during the day, the teas can be used and very good results are obtained. All the herbs mentioned above can be used as teas.

Parasitic infestations

Parasitic infestations are still commonly encountered in general practice, the most common being head lice and threadworms. They persist despite the development of potent chemical treatments because they are easily transmitted from person to person, and effective treatment has to be aimed at the whole household rather than just the affected individual. In the case of head lice in schoolchildren, re-infestation is highly likely because close contact is a daily occurrence. There can be few families that have not received a warning from the school authorities regarding a problem with head lice. There are few symptoms; usually just itching of the scalp, particularly behind the ears. Head lice rarely cause serious harm, although there is still a social stigma associated with infestation. Treatment is related to the insect's life cycle. The adults lay their eggs close to the scalp, where it is warmest and the eggs are least likely to be dislodged. After 7–10 days they hatch, leaving behind the familiar 'nits', which are the empty egg cases. The best way to spot lice is by means of a fine toothed comb when the hair is wet. The young lice will be caught between the teeth.

There are three main groups of insecticides used in the UK: the *BNF* lists malathion preparations, those based on synthetic pyrethroids (permethrin and phenothrin), and carbaryl preparations. Since 1996 the latter have only been available on prescription, since they have been found to be carcinogenic in rodents when used over a long period of time. Current clinical practice had concluded that only permethrin was an effective treatment; however, soon after this it was reported that there was widespread resistance to it. Another interesting factor was also highlighted; it was found that chlorine can inactivate some of the insecticides, and swimming should therefore be avoided on the day before application. It could well be an important factor in the success of a treatment.

Particularly worrying was the finding that traces of the insecticides used in treatment shampoos and lotions were being detected in the urine, having been absorbed via the scalp. This is hardly surprising, since it is recommended that lotions be applied to the hair at night and left on for 12 hours. This is to ensure that the insects are exposed to a high concentration of pediculicide over a long period of time. It also ensures that a considerable amount diffuses into the blood. Public concern regarding the use of powerful insecticides has highlighted the role of herbal medicine in treating infestations, and parents are actively seeking safer alternatives to the insecticides mentioned above. At Wapping, it has been found that a combination of tea tree oil and lavender oil (used in equal proportions) is highly effective for the treatment of head lice. This is certainly not the only mixture of essential oils that will work, and there are many different variations on this. Not only are the oils pleasant to use, but there is no danger of them being absorbed through the skin. They are only left in contact with the hair for 10 minutes, and are then shampooed out. As an additional precaution, a rinse consisting of a weak alcoholic solution of *Artemisia absinthium* (wormwood) has also been employed. As the common name of this plant suggests, it is an age-old remedy for invertebrate infestations. When taken orally, wormwood is also very useful for the treatment of threadworm infestations in children – avoiding the need for mebendazole or piperazine.

Eczema

Atopic eczema is a common condition, affecting approximately 10 per cent of schoolchildren (David, 1995). In addition to the characteristic inflamed skin lesions and changes in skin structure brought about by intra-epidermal oedema and hyperkeratosis, the associated scratching is a major problem. Not only does it further damage the skin, but it also disturbs the sleep of both the sufferer and his or her family. A child with severe eczema can seriously disrupt the life of the whole family. Its course is remarkably unpredictable, and fluctuations can occur on a day-to-day basis. At this health centre, cases are often referred by the health visitors. Parents become concerned when they find that repeated applications of steroid creams or ointments only work for a short while. They are frequently seeking a 'natural' treatment for their child's eczema, and this provides the first contact with the medical herbalist.

As in the case of any referral, a detailed past history is taken and diet once again highlighted. The parent may well just want a 'herbal cream', but this is never given in isolation. It is very important that this is prescribed within the holistic framework; only then will the cream be most effective. If a child is on a very poor diet, then the cream is merely masking the true triggers. It is important to point out to the parents that although triggers are factors that exacerbate the eczema, they do not cause it. By considering the most common trigger factors, it is possible to lessen the severity of the eczema and reduce the child's daily discomfort.

One of the most important factors is the use of biological washing powders. To date, at Wapping Health Centre, not one patient has been able to explain the actual difference between biological and non-biological washing powders in terms of their content. They are totally unaware that biological powders contain active proteases (protein-digesting enzymes) and should never be used to wash the clothing or bedding of a child with eczema. Fabric conditioners and stain removers should likewise be avoided. The problem is magnified in those households where there is no washing machine and items are hand-washed. It is very difficult to removes residues of powder effectively when rinsing by hand.

It is regularly reported in medical journals that there is no evidence that diet influences the progression of eczema. To an extent this is perfectly true; there does not appear to be a specific set of foods known to aggravate the condition. However, there is no doubt that there are several chemical substances that do exacerbate it. This has become evident from a detailed record of the patients' diets at Wapping. In general, a large proportion of foods aimed directly at the 4–10 year age group are highly coloured and highly flavoured. In all cases, when these foods are replaced with realistic alternatives, the severity of the eczema decreases. Where, for instance, a child is eating one or two packets of flavoured crisps every day, the parent is advised to replace these with the ready-salted version. Similarly, where large quantities of brightly coloured and strongly flavoured 'fruit' drinks are being ingested, more healthy fruit cordials are suggested. A particularly worrying feature of children's drinks is the promotion of the 'low sugar' varieties, and this is already highlighted in Chapter 4. It is bad enough that drinks marketed at adults have artificial sweeteners added to non-diet products, but it is alarming to find such high levels of artificial sweeteners in children's drinks. Of course the dental aspect is promoted, and these products are all described as being 'kind to teeth'. But how kind are they to a developing digestive system? Experiences with adults with IBS suggest that we could well be creating a future generation of adults with assorted gastrointestinal problems. Children need natural sugar, as long as it is not taken in excessive amounts. If dental hygiene is encouraged and the teeth are brushed regularly, there is no problem; the only exception to this is where drinks are given in feeding bottles to very young children, and a sugary solution is therefore in constant contact with the teeth. This practice will cause serious decay, and should be discouraged. At Wapping, an interesting observation has been made regarding a link between childhood eczema and saccharin. On several occasions a child's eczema has healed using a topical application and dietary modification, only for the parents to telephone and report a sudden flare-up. Careful questioning reveals that they have recently been prescribed a saccharin-based paediatric analgesic or antibiotic suspension. The trend is now towards replacing sugar-based children's medicines with saccharin-based versions. However, special consideration should be given to this when a child suffers from an allergic condition.

The type of milk that an infant is receiving is bound to be a factor for consideration when investigating eczema. The condition is rarer in those children who are breast-fed for several months. It is often observed that eczema suddenly increases in severity at weaning, and it may be the case that a child has a sensitivity to cow's milk. It is important to be certain of this before attempting to modify the diet, but it is possible to substitute goat's milk if this allergy has been positively identified. Despite a lower lactose level and certain differences in the amounts of some inorganic ions, the two milks are overall very similar (Paul and Southgate, 1976). To avoid any possibility of mineral deficiencies, however, it is best to use goat's milk after weaning, when other foods will provide an alternative source. For older children with this allergy, several supermarkets produce detailed booklets listing guaranteed milk-free items, making it a little easier to be certain that milk is not accidentally included in their diet.

Where the eczema is severe and dietary modification alone is not sufficient to control it, topical medication is offered. A large proportion of parents actively express concern regarding the repeated application of steroids (David, 1987), and there is indeed a risk of breakdown of skin structure, which makes healing more and more difficult. Another danger that has been highlighted is the impairment of growth in children with atopic eczema, although the link with long-term topical steroid use is tentative (Kristmundsdottir and David, 1987). The application of herbal creams has proved very successful. Three main species have produced the best results: *Calendula officinalis* (marigold), *Echinacea angustifolia* (cone flower) and *Matricaria recutita* (German chamomile).

Chamomile is a very versatile herb. It can safely be given to very young children as a tea, in a drinking bottle, thus allowing it to exert its anti-inflammatory properties systemically. It is, however, very important to instruct the parents in how to make the tea properly; some of the anti-inflammatory compounds are volatile, and thus it should be made in a covered vessel such as a teapot, using either the routinely available tea bags or the loose dried herb. It should be allowed to infuse for at least 5 minutes, and then cooled. It is also perfectly safe to rinse the skin of babies with the cooled diluted tea at the end of their normal bath-time; its anti-inflammatory action is very soothing, especially before bed. Similarly, it can be applied to the skin using cotton wool, where scratching has become severe. If there is also seborrhoeic eczema, the chamomile tea should be used as a final rinse whenever the hair is shampooed.

The most successful treatment at this centre has been the Calendula cream, applied freely. The more frequently it is applied and the better it is rubbed into the skin, the greater the improvement. Older children are said to dislike topical treatment (David, 1995). However, it has become clear that, if they are provided with their own 'special' pot of herbal cream, they will eagerly take on the responsibility of applying the cream – not least of all because they come to understand that it is effective in helping them. These children are seen regularly, and praised for their efforts towards their own treatment.

The cream containing *Calendula officinalis* has another very valuable advantage in that it has considerable antifungal and antibacterial activity. Since secondary infection is common in eczema, the regular application of this cream confers protection against infection. In most cases the causative organism is identified as *Staphylococcus aureus*, although in severe flare-ups some of the beta-haemolytic streptococci may also be identified (David and Cambridge, 1986). The usual treatment would be a course of antibiotics. In the case of a staphylococcal infection the drug of choice would normally be flucloxacillin, which not only has a particularly unpleasant taste but must also be taken four times daily. This in itself is often distressing to a child, and the treatment also has all the usual disadvantages of antibiotics.

Eczematous skin is often very dry, so treatment usually includes the application of emollients in order to attempt to reduce loss of water over the surface of the skin. A considerable amount of water can leave via the damaged epidermis, and substances can also gain entry through it. For example, allergens can enter and give rise to an allergic eczema. Application of the cream containing *Echinacea angustifolia* usually keeps the skin well moisturized, and avoids the necessity of having to apply other preparations. The overall aim is to maintain healthy skin structure and thus promote healing; it must be remembered that in severe eczema the barrier function of the skin is overwhelmed, and following immersion in water during bathing, osmotic function can be disturbed. This feature has led to the development of silicone-based barrier creams, which repel water and replace the usual physiological function.

As far as oral medication is concerned, it is preferable to avoid the stronger alcoholic tinctures in children under 8 years of age. There are of course exceptions to this rule; for example, if persistent infection is a problem, an antibacterial tincture is far preferable to yet another course of antibiotics. Children with eczema are usually only offered the chamomile tea mentioned above. If they will take it from a bottle, its sedative properties are an advantage and it will help them have a relaxed sleep. It is also effective in mild colic, as it is a good gut relaxant. Where the child is being breast-fed, it can be given to the mother. Not only will some of its active principles be secreted in the milk for the benefit of the baby, but the mother will also greatly benefit from its general relaxant properties. In allopathic circles, it is common for children with eczema to be prescribed sedative antihistamines, and one of those commonly prescribed is trimeprazine (Savin *et al.*, 1979). They have no effect on the actual eczema, and are simply being used for their sedative side effect, which is undesirable.

The approach in adults with eczema is similar, with diet being the central consideration. As more and more cases are studied, definite 'suspect' food items come to light. If these are sequentially removed from the diet, the main cause of the adverse reaction can often be identified. For example, there have been several cases where pork has been implicated. It is not necessarily the actual protein that is the allergenic substance; apparently the pig receives a mixture of several antibiotics prior to slaughter, and it could well be the residues of these drugs that cause the reaction in some people. Flare-ups are often directly related to stress, so this needs to be borne in mind.

A tincture is often required, and will utilize herbs traditionally used in the treatment of skin conditions, such as *Echinacea angustifolia* (cone flower), together with those that improve eliminative functions – i.e. they act on the liver. Two of the latter are *Arctium lappa* (burdock) and *Rumex crispus* (yellow dock). An anti-inflammatory agent may also be utilized, such as *Glycyrrhiza glabra* (liquorice) or *Matricaria recutita* (German chamomile). Where anxiety is a predominant feature, relaxant herbs can also be included. The creams have proved very popular indeed, to the extent that many women prefer to use them in place of moisturizing cosmetic preparations. This not only reduces the chance of irritation by unnecessary chemicals, but additionally confers protection against secondary infection.

Rheumatoid arthritis

Rheumatoid arthritis is a chronic inflammatory systemic disorder; unlike osteoarthritis, its effects are not restricted to the joints. The characteristic inflammatory lesions may occur in a variety of tissues, including the lungs, heart, skin, eyes and salivary glands; however, its effect on the joints is commonly the most disabling feature. Its progression is due to a series of changes brought about by a complex

series of immunological reactions. The trigger for the changes is not always obvious; a variety of micro-organisms have been implicated, but cultures of synovial fluid taken from severely inflamed joints are usually sterile. It has been suggested that macrophages associated with the synovium bring about the inflammatory response. They have been found to possess a high level of iron, originating from small intra-articular haemorrhages, and if iron becomes reduced to the ferrous form the production of free radicles is stimulated. These free radicals damage fatty acid molecules, which are a major component of cell membranes, thus causing damage at the cell level. It has also been established that T-lymphocytes outnumber B-lymphocytes in the cellular infiltrate of rheumatoid synovium. The cytokines released by these cells could have marked effects on a whole range of cells including macrophages, osteoclasts, osteoblasts, chondrocytes and joint capsule fibroblasts. Immunological abnormalities also extend to the humoral aspects of immune function. In general, patients with severe rheumatoid arthritis have high titres of rheumatoid factor, which can usually be demonstrated in the plasma cells of the synovium of affected joints. By contrast, seronegative individuals can show mild forms of the disease. There is also evidence that aggregations of the immune complexes trigger acute inflammatory responses in a range of tissues.

The allopathic approach attempts to slow down the progression of the disease by the administration of immunosuppressive agents and corticosteroids, and the use of disease modifying anti-rheumatic drugs (DMARDs). Symptomatic relief of pain is administered via non-steroidal anti-inflammatory drugs, which also reduce inflammation. The latter act by inhibiting the cyclo-oxygenase (COX) enzymes involved in prostaglandin synthesis. Recent studies have revealed that there are at least two cyclo-oxygenase enzymes (COX-1 and COX-2). The first is thought to be responsible for maintaining normal functioning of the gastric mucosa (Choy, 1997), so any interference with its activity is highly undesirable. COX-2 is thought to be directly involved with the inflammatory response. Because of this division of function, research has been centred on the development of inhibitors that are specific for COX-2, in order to reduce damage to the gastric mucosa; meloxicam preferentially inhibits COX-2. The NSAIDS can be very effective in pain control, but they simply provide symptomatic relief and do nothing to reduce the progression of the disease. The DMARDs are employed to help with the latter; the mechanisms of their actions are unknown. They include substances such as methotrexate, sulphasalazine, penicillamine and gold, and several anti-malarial drugs – for example, hydroxychloroquine. Immunosuppressants include corticosteroids, cyclosporin, azathioprine and cyclophosphamide (Watson, 1998). Cyclosporin first gained its licence for treating patients who did not benefit from other approaches to treatment in the 1990s, but renal toxicity remains a concern (Chadhuri *et al.*, 1997). The toxicity of several other drugs in this category has been a cause for questioning; for example, the hepatotoxicity of methotrexate (Weinblatt, 1996), and eye damage caused by anti-malarials (Conaghan and Brooks, 1997).

There is by no means a standard allopathic treatment approach for rheumatoid arthritis, although the most popular approach is currently combination therapy. A recent survey of 200 rheumatologists revealed that the great majority used combination therapy, the most common (39 per cent) being methotrexate combined with either hydroxychloroquine or sulphasalazine (O'Dell, 1997). The historical claim that rheumatoid arthritis is triggered by an infective process is actively being reinvestigated. The allopathic approach once included treatment with antibiotics such as minocycline (O'Dell *et al.*, 1997). The early course of the disease involves an interaction between macrophages and T-cells, followed by a large release of cytokine. This causes the resultant inflammation, and consequent tissue damage. The latest research is considering the development of anti-cytokine treatments. It has already been reported that inflammation is markedly reduced when antibodies to tumour necrosis factor (TNF) are administered (Muller-Ladner, 1996).

The treatment of rheumatoid arthritis (RA) using herbs has a long tradition. There are a large number of herbs that have been utilized to treat this disorder, many of which have now been shown to have a range of compounds that are anti-inflammatory in action. There has been much interest at Wapping Health Centre regarding the treatment of this condition using herbal medicine, and many patients are now well controlled using solely a herbal tincture. Just how successful treatment is depends on how far the disease has progressed at the time of the initial consultation. The overall aims of the treatment are to reduce active inflammation and pain, and thus minimize joint damage.

As with many disorders, several restrictive diets have been proposed. However, as previously noted, despite the plethora of books aimed at controlling RA by dietary modification, there is not a standard diet that offers relief to the majority of sufferers. Many patients will become aware of certain foods that seem to aggravate the condition, the most common being dairy products and caffeine. In others, however, the exclusion of these makes little difference. It is worthwhile mentioning the role of diet in the condition, so that the individual is able to make an informed decision as to whether to try an exclusion diet for a few weeks. The herbs used act to reduce inflammation and stimulate immune function. The most frequently prescribed species at Wapping are *Apium graveolens* (celery), *Salix alba* (white willow), *Glycyrrhiza glabra* (liquorice), *Harpagophytum procumbens* (devil's claw), *Menyanthes trifoliata* (bogbean) and *Matricaria recutita* (German chamomile). In addition to this group of herbs, which are principally anti-inflammatory in action, others that might be used include *Echinacea angustifolia* (cone flower), for its action on the immune system, *Galium aparine* (cleavers), for its stimulatory effect on the lymphatic system, and *Arctium lappa* (burdock) or *Rumex crispus* (yellow dock), to stimulate the eliminatory fuction of the liver. There are many patients at Wapping who are very well maintained on a prescription containing a selection of these herbs. The aim is always to achieve as low a dose as possible; in several cases just one 5 ml dose per day is sufficient to control the pain, whereas others require three doses per day. The long-term prescription of predominantly anti-inflammatory tinctures may well provide protection against some of the systemic features of rheumatoid arthritis, but further research is required in this area.

Pre-menstrual syndrome and dysmenorrhoea

Women with pre-menstrual syndrome (PMS) and dysmenorrhoea are frequently referred for herbal treatment. There is obviously a wide range of causes for PMS, and the long consultation time enables the causative factors to be fully investigated. Where it is probable that there is a hormonal imbalance, herbal medicine has a very interesting type of treatment to offer, there being no allopathic equivalent. An extract of *Vitex agnus-castus* (chasteberry) may be given. This is a very valuable herb, since its action is directed at altering the ratio of oestrogen to progesterone. It acts at the level of the anterior pituitary, causing a decrease in the production of follicle-stimulating hormone (FSH) and an increase in the secretion of luteinizing hormone (LH). The overall result is that there is a shift towards increased production of progesterone. Research dating from the 1960s, where female guinea pigs given extracts of Vitex, showed increased development of corpora lutea and proliferation of mammary gland tissue, which would appear to be consistent with this observation. Uterine weight and follicular development were slightly decreased (Haller, 1961). The first large-scale clinical trial was reported in 1954 by Probst and Roth, who noted marked improvement in patients suffering from dysfunctional uterine bleeding brought about by cystic hyperplasia of the endometrium.

This condition is due to a deficiency of progesterone, so the results again point to the progesteronic action of Vitex. Because it acts by altering the balance between oestrogen and progesterone, it can be employed in the treatment of a wide range of menstrual disorders; Bleier (1959) reports success with polymenorrhoea, oligomenorrhoea and menorrhagia.

The fact that the majority of women suffering from PMS experience a decrease in the intensity of their symptoms with Vitex would fit in with the theory that PMS is caused by a shortage of progesterone. It would also support research that suggests that it results from hyperoestrogenism. At Wapping, Vitex has been found to be very successful in controlling PMS. On several occasions, symptoms which individual women had found particularly distressing – for example, arthralgia – completely resolved following a course of Vitex. Where Vitex is appropriate, it is far superior to an allopathic treatment that must rely on the administration of hormones, with all the associated side effects. Where a woman is offered the contraceptive pill not for its contraceptive action, but for its possible role in reducing the pain of dysmenorrhoea, it would be far better to consider the use of Vitex.

As can be imagined, Vitex provides a realistic alternative to those women who have decided against hormone replacement therapy (HRT) but who do require relief from menopausal symptoms. It may be taken alone, or in conjunction with those species that effectively suppress hot flushes – for example, *Salvia officinalis* (sage). The beneficial effects of this herb have been known throughout the ages, and there are many references to it being taken regularly as a tea by menopausal women. In the form of the more potent tincture, very small doses are sufficient to bring about a clinically beneficial effect.

Conditions affecting the respiratory system

Reference to the respiratory system cannot be omitted; infections within this system are one of the commonest reasons for a GP consultation. Of the 600 upper respiratory infections that the average GP sees per annum, about 25 per cent involve a sore throat (Palmer, 1992). The medical herbalist has several effective remedies to offer, including tincture of myrrh (*Commiphora molmol*), which is not only a potent anti-bacterial agent but is also very warming and soothing. It is administered undiluted, and can be used as a gargle, or a few drops may be swallowed. This tincture is also highly effective in clearing up mouth ulcers. A good demulcent agent for sore throats is thyme and liquorice syrup. Where there is evidence of bacterial infection, a range of herbs can be used; perhaps the best known is *Thymus vulgaris* (common thyme). In order to improve lymphatic function, *Galium aparine* (cleavers) is included in most upper respiratory tinctures, together with a more general immune system stimulant such as *Echinacea angustifolia* (cone flower). Both these herbs are also anti-inflammatory in action, and Echinacea is another herb that can be used as a component of a gargle. Depending on the precise symptomatology, various other species may be included. For example, where phlegm needs loosening, a herb with a strong expectorant action – such as *Plantago major* (plantain) – would be incorporated. This herb has been shown to increase the rate of ciliary action in the brush border epithelium of the respiratory tract, so removing mucus more efficiently. As the Latin root of its name (tussis: a cough) indicates, *Tussilago farfara* (coltsfoot) is a relaxing expectorant and anti-catarrhal. In order to suppress a hacking cough, the syrup of *Prunus serotina* (wild cherry bark) may be given. There are many other herbs that may be utilized for conditions of the respiratory system; several demonstrate their potent effects due to the fact that some of the active principles (for example volatile oils) are excreted over the surface of the lung, exerting their action as they pass across the cells. This effect is particularly well known for one very strong antibacterial herb – garlic.

Irritable bowel syndrome

> Men are of different constitutions with respect to their powers of digestion, nor less different with respect to the irritability of their system, and are consequently variously affected by the same ailment: and this so much as to have produced the vulgar observation that one man's meat is another man's poison.
>
> William Cullen, 1789

In order to fully appreciate why this disorder responds so well to herbal medicine, it is necessary to review the main characteristics of the condition and the way it is managed within primary health care.

Irritable bowel syndrome (IBS) is reported to affect up to 15 per cent of the adult population in western countries (Heaton, 1994), the incidence amongst females being approximately twice as high as that amongst males. It would appear to be equally prevalent in China (Bi-Zhen and Qi-Ying, 1988), although less common in Southeast Asia. Many of those suffering from the condition do not seek medical help (Bommelaer *et al.*, 1986). Its aetiology is unknown, and it is a complex multifactorial condition which gives rise to a range of gastrointestinal symptoms. The main feature characterizing it is, as the name suggests, an increase in gut sensitivity, giving rise to inappropriately strong nervous responses to both chemical and physical stimuli. Psychiatry still perceives it as a principally psychogenic disorder and, on a more general level, psychological factors such as stress are recognized as being important in some individuals.

There are no diagnostic tests for the condition, so it has always been difficult to define. However, in 1989 a set of guidelines was published, which attempted to make the diagnosis more standardized. These became known as the Rome criteria for the diagnosis of IBS. They specify that the following symptoms must occur continuously (or recurrently) for at least 3 months:

1. Abdominal pain relieved by defecation or associated with a change in frequency or consistency of the stool, and/or
2. Defecation disturbed by two or more of the following:
   a. altered stool frequency
   b. altered stool form
   c. altered stool passage (straining, urgency, feeling of incomplete defecation)
   d. passage of mucus
3. Bloating or a feeling of abdominal distension, which usually accompany the above.

Given the vast array of presentations of the condition, as reflected by the term 'syndrome', there can be no single remedy appropriate for the treatment of IBS. Klein (1988) summarizes the situation thus:

> It is concluded that not a single study offers convincing evidence that any therapy is effective in treating the IBS symptom complex.

The allopathic approach is to select the most distressing symptom and prescribe for this. Should diarrhoea feature, then an appropriate anti-diarrhoeal agent is given. Opioid agents such as loperamide and codeine, as well as diphenoxylate, are preferred. These agents decrease bowel motility by the inhibition of acetylcholine release. Loperamide is the most commonly prescribed drug, since it exhibits poor penetration of the blood–brain barrier and thus the incidence of CNS side effects is very low. This feature contributed to its associated risk–benefit ratio that allowed it to become an over-the-counter medicine. It is effective in decreasing intestinal transit and increasing uptake of water and ions, and also increases tone of the rectal sphincter muscles, thereby improving faecal incontinence where this is a problem (Cann *et al.*, 1984). The administration of enteric coated capsules of peppermint oil, which release their contents in the region of the small intestine, has often been claimed to have antispasmodic effects. However, most studies have reported an effect only slightly greater than a placebo. Although peppermint oil might be thought of as a herbal medicine, it is not, because it is not the whole-plant extract. Generally speaking, an oil such as this would be considered too harsh for internal administration – in fact, it would be particularly inappropriate for IBS, where the overall characterization of the condition includes an over-sensitivity to chemical stimuli. If mint were selected as a herbal medicine, it would be given as the usual alcohol-based tincture – which is, of course, an extract of the whole plant, and therefore contains only a very small amount of the oil. Mint has not featured in the treatment of any of the IBS cases at Wapping Health Centre. Another way of approaching treatment is by the use of muscarinic antagonists, such as atropine, propantheline, and dicyclomine. However, all are poorly selective in action, and they tend to produce anticholinergic side effects such as blurred vision, dry mouth and arrhythmias. For this reason, such drugs are available on prescription only.

Patients have commonly tried an antispasmodic such as alverine or mebeverine. There are very few data available on the efficacy of alverine and, as the Pharmaceutical Society points out (Pharmaceutical Journal Practice Checklist, 1997), 'its continued use is justified essentially only on its long history of safe use'. Interestingly, this is a privilege not afforded to most herbal medicines that come with an even longer history of safe use. Mebeverine is generally found to have a marginally better effect than a placebo (Pharmaceutical Journal Practice Checklist, 1997). The main advantage of these two compounds is that, since they are selective for smooth muscle of the gut, there is an absence of anticholinergic side effects. Both are available as over-the-counter medicines and therefore, by the time patients consult a medical herbalist, it is most likely that they have tried one or more of the above preparations. Since IBS is multifactorial and consists of a variable number of different symptoms, this approach can, at best, only be expected to provide occasional symptomatic relief. Much research has been carried out on IBS, not least because it accounts for a large percentage of GP consultation time and a correspondingly large prescription budget. Those with IBS account for 25–50 per cent of referrals to gastroenterologists.

The most striking characteristic about the typical approach to treatment is a lack of consideration of diet. It is well known that the gut is over-sensitive, yet the most likely factor to trigger this over-sensitivity, namely food, is very rarely considered in research papers dealing with the approach to treatment. This is entirely understandable, since the effect of diet would not be a standard one – a fact recognized by the eighteenth century physician William Cullen, as illustrated in the quote above. It is not a case of trying to find one type of food responsible for causing or contributing to IBS in general; there is undoubtedly a different trigger factor in every case. The only real attention that has been focused on diet is with respect to fibre. This is because, historically, a 'high fibre' diet has been associated with healthy peristalsis and, in particular, colon activity. Thus, if a general recommendation regarding diet has to be made for IBS sufferers, this is felt to be the most appropriate. It is also considered to be easy advice for patients to follow, and highly likely to relieve some of the symptoms.

It is also worth noting that a recent study suggests that up to 50 per cent of patients diagnosed with IBS are in fact exhibiting food intolerance. If this is indeed the case, then it becomes essential to consider diet in detail.

IBS and the herbalist

IBS is the commonest functional disorder of the gastrointestinal system, yet it is not well managed within primary health care. It has been suggested that it is the failure of allopathic medicine to meet patients' needs that has resulted in one-third of IBS patients seeking help from 'alternative' practitioners (Smart *et al.*, 1986). Because it is so complex a condition, with a highly variable presentation, it needs to be addressed by an equally variable means of treatment. The symptomatic approach will never be successful because there are so many different symptoms, and the typical patient returns to the GP *ad infinitum*, dealing with the various symptoms in progression. That it responds so well to treatment by herbal medicine is hardly surprising, given the detailed enquiry into diet, the long consultation time and the individually formulated prescriptions, which can be modified according to any change in symptoms.

Assuming that the past medical history does not point to a serious pathology, and suspicious symptoms such as constant abdominal pain, weight loss, or passage of blood via the rectum have been fully investigated, the herbalist will attempt to identify the underlying cause of the various symptoms. The label of 'IBS' is no longer important. Indeed, it has often been pointed out that it is simply an umbrella term for functional gut disorders of unknown aetiology that fit the Rome criteria. Once full details of the symptoms within the digestive system have been ascertained, and the diet diary has been examined, the treatment can begin. It is the over-sensitivity of the gut, principally to food but also to changes in hormone levels (for example during the menstrual cycle) and to stress, that is the main consideration. Generally speaking, the treatment of a patient diagnosed with 'IBS' proceeds as follows:

1. A detailed case history is taken
2. The diet diary is examined, and potentially 'suspect' foods are discussed
3. A review of diet modifications is carried out
4. Herbal medicine is prescribed (if required).

Perhaps one of the most important points to note is that herbal medicine is never prescribed at the first consultation. As already pointed out in Chapter 4, if the diet is changed and a herbal tincture is prescribed at the same time, this can only confuse the issue; it will be impossible to assess the relative contributions of dietary change and herbal medicine to the changes in symptoms.

It is certainly the case at Wapping Health Centre that, by the time patients with IBS consult the medical herbalist, they have been told somewhere along the line to follow a 'high fibre' diet. Usually this is where the dietary advice ends, so frequently patients earnestly seek out all foods promoted as being 'high fibre', and these foods feature regularly in the diet diary of a patient with IBS. The high incidence of IBS amongst the population has undoubtedly been the catalyst in marketing these foods. The trouble is that many processed foods are the wrong type of high fibre foods, and they can and do aggravate symptoms in many individuals. For example, harsh breakfast cereals, commonly high in added bran, are frequently found to increase abdominal pain. When this type of product is replaced by a breakfast cereal that is 'softer' in texture (for example, cornflakes or porridge), an immediate improvement follows.

Much education is needed; fibre is present as cellulose in every plant cell wall, so fresh plant material such as fruits and vegetables, with their additional high water content (which also helps prevent constipation), are the best sources of fibre for a sensitive digestive system. Ingestion of large amounts of harsh high fibre breakfast cereal is akin to passing sawdust through the digestive system, and about as nutritious. It is ironic that the very people who are trying to help themselves in purchasing 'high fibre' foods are those whose digestive systems cannot cope with such material, and they would be far better off on an 'ordinary' cereal. It is also relevant to note that most people, when questioned, have virtually no idea what fibre actually is. They are therefore unable to seek out natural sources for themselves, and come to rely on the highly reassuring packaging of the 'high fibre' foods marketed as being good for the digestive system.

By taking in fresh plant material, a whole range of naturally synthesized vitamins will be ingested, as well as minerals that the plant has absorbed from the soil. Patients are advised to take in as wide a range of plant species as possible, and to include as many different plant parts as possible (stems, leaves, roots, flowers, fruits, seeds, etc.). By doing this, it is ensured that the widest range of nutrients will be encountered, since each botanical part performs a different function and is of a different biochemical composition. If patients need help in planning such a varied input, the information is written down for them in their diet diaries at the time of consultation. There are a few plant products, however, that may have to be avoided in IBS, although this is not the case for every individual. The stone cells of pears, which give them their characteristic 'gritty' texture, can make them irritant, so patients should be asked whether they have a problem with this particular fruit. For those who do, it is reassuring for them to know that there is a good biological reason. Likewise, wholegrain (not wholemeal) bread can also be irritant to a sensitive digestive tract. Other seeds can also pose a problem – for example nuts, which if not chewed sufficiently can be 'sharp' on the mucosa. All patients benefit from the kind of general dietary advice outlined in Chapter 4. Essentially, they need to reduce their intake of processed foods (which are high in additives) and cut down on all those foods of doubtful content. This includes all poor quality meat items such as pies and pasties, and low-grade mincemeat and sausages. Items such as 'vegetable oil' should also be avoided because, like the above products, they are of variable composition (that is a mixture of several different seed oils). By sticking to one named pure source of oil, for example sunflower oil, yet one more variable is cut out. For the same reason, butter is infinitely preferable to all the 'vegetable based' spreads. These measures dramatically reduce the range of artificial additives entering the digestive tract, any of which are potentially capable of irritating a sensitive digestive system. Patients are advised to eat easily digested meat such as chicken and other white meat, and to avoid pork and beef, which are heavier on the digestive system. Since fish is also a good source of protein, they are also asked to consider including more of this in the diet. In addition to fresh fish, canned salmon, tuna, pilchards and sardines are useful items in the diet, although canned foods in general are to be avoided due to their reduced vitamin content. It must be made clear that all the foods ingested must be recorded in the diet diary, since some of the most 'irritant' foods are some snacks. Often it initially appears that an individual is eating a very healthy background balanced diet, with all home-cooked food, etc. However, when questioned more closely, it may be found that they are snacking on items that are highly likely to cause the symptoms they describe. One such patient was found to be eating, in addition to her otherwise excellent diet, two packets of prawn cocktail flavoured potato crisps every day. In the case of this particular individual, they were undoubtedly a contributory factor to the IBS symptoms, and this was easily demonstrated by her marked improvement when they were withdrawn. As may be imagined, such a minor point can so easily be missed. Given that even a cursory look at diet is not the rule in the treatment of IBS, how are such idiosyncratic reactions going to be identified in the majority of patients? At Wapping, time and time again, it is the minute attention to detail that has been the key to successful treatment. This is one reason why so many people do not need a herbal tincture; dietary modification alone is often sufficient. In some cases some of the symptoms may persist, albeit at a much lower intensity – for example bloating. In this case, tablets of *Ulmus fulva* (slippery elm) are prescribed. For those who prefer, it may also be taken in its original powdered form and made into a drink. At Wapping, this has been the single most effective treatment for IBS where it has been necessary to prescribe. Slippery elm has a very long history of use in the treatment of a variety of gastrointestinal disorders. It is a particularly safe herb, being composed (as its common name suggests) mainly of mucilagenous polysaccharides, and can be given to young children and babies. In North America it was once used as a weaning gruel when food supplies were low. Because of the relatively high molecular weights of the polysaccharide components, they stay mainly within the gut, and only small amounts of monosaccharides are absorbed into the bloodstream. Thus, interactions with other medications are not a problem. The overall effect of Ulmus is to soothe any irritation and allow healing to proceed under a protective mucilagenous layer; it is therefore best taken as a complete course over a period of approximately one month.

Approximately 60–70 per cent of patients are treated either with diet modification alone, or diet modification in combination with *Ulmus fulva* (slippery elm). As far as the prescription of tinctures is concerned, their composition is highly variable and depends on the dominant symptoms. Where a smooth muscle relaxant is indicated, *Viburnum opulus* (cramp bark) is commonly employed. *Matricaria recutita* (German chamomile) is a good general gut relaxant, and this may also be prescribed as a tea for infants with colic. Where a soothing demulcent is required, *Althaea officinalis* RADIX, which is rich in mucilages, is prescribed. *Filipendula ulmaria* (meadowsweet) is often included where there is hyperacidity, and it is also antibacterial.

Taken as a group, IBS patients show three common types of symptoms. Firstly, there is usually abdominal pain, most commonly in the right or left iliac fossa (or both). Frequently it is reported that passage of flatus or defecation relieves this. At least 70 per cent of patients interviewed at Wapping Health Centre describe bloating as a major problem. It is usually a physical effect, rather than just a sensation of 'heaviness', and sufferers will describe how they have to loosen their clothing. Finally, there is disturbed bowel habit, which is highly variable in form. Two common observations are that constipation is more common in females, and that diarrhoea occurs more often in the morning. The most frequently reported symptom, bloating, is the one that is not only directly linked to abdominal pain, but is also the one that disappears first when dietary changes are implemented and slippery elm is administered. When investigating patients' symptoms, full details of the digestive process are recorded, including ingestion. It has been found that when the processing of food in the mouth is considered, at least 50 per cent of those reporting bloating as a major problem are those who do not chew their food sufficiently. This occurs for a variety of reasons; for example, it may be due to absence of molars or to painful dental conditions. Most commonly, however, it is due to poor eating habits, where the food is 'bolted' and swallowed quickly. Not only does this mean that a reduced surface area of food is presented to the digestive enzymes, but it also results in more air being swallowed. Because the enzymes are unable to complete digestion fully, the overall efficiency of digestion is reduced. Disturbed digestion and trapped air result in bloating, which in turn leads to abdominal pain.

The importance of psychological factors in IBS is difficult to ascertain. It has frequently been concluded that those diagnosed with IBS have greater symptomatic and physiologic responses to assorted stress factors than healthy individuals (Kumar and Wingate, 1985), or a higher frequency of psychiatric diagnoses such as anxiety (Walker *et al.*, 1990) or depression (Heefer *et al.*, 1978). However, these conclusions are questionable, since such patients have all been selected and referred for psychiatric assessment. It is likely that the overall incidence of psychiatric disorders within IBS is approximately the same as within the general population. Undoubtedly there will be some individuals who are more likely to seek help, and this subset of patients may include those who are undergoing a greater level of stress than others – for example following loss of employment, bereavement, etc. Much research concludes that one of the most important factors in treatment is a strong patient–practitioner relationship (Drossman and Thompson, 1992), and it is therefore hardly surprising that those with severe IBS symptoms find psychotherapy far more helpful than a range of pharmaceutical preparations (Svedlund *et al.*, 1983). The human factor – a listening ear – is all-important. However, from a herbalist's point of view, in IBS any type of counselling should always be accompanied by a consideration of diet.

An interesting case history

The following case history has been included to illustrate how versatile herbal medicine can be. It is not a case that would typically be referred for treatment by herbal medicine, yet the results speak for themselves.

A 36-year-old woman with Crohn's disease had been experiencing considerable difficulties following an ileostomy that had been performed 18 months earlier. There was constant leaking from the ileostomy bags, which resulted in disturbed sleep and poor energy levels during the day. The patient was exhausted and, with a young family to look after, she was keen to consider any treatment that might take a fresh look at her problems. She was advised by the Practice Nurse to make an appointment with the medical herbalist. After a full medical history had been taken, it was decided to focus on the problem that was causing her most concern – namely, the leaking from the ileostomy bag. It was evident that, since there was little that could be done about a poorly formed stoma, we would have to concentrate on altering the nature of the effluent. By attempting to make it more viscous, it was hoped that leaking would be decreased, allowing the patient to gain a full night's sleep. The properties of *Ulmus fulva* (slippery elm) seemed to be ideal. It is well known for its great water-holding properties and, as previously outlined, it is a very safe herb that can be administered long-term. This was an important factor in the treatment of this particular patient; it was likely that she would be taking any herbs prescribed continuously. The Ulmus was prescribed in the powdered form, to be taken as a drink three times a day. Within 48 hours, the patient had reported a very marked improvement. In her follow-up appointment 2 weeks later, she described how she had only been woken twice during the fortnight, whereas previously she had woken an average of three times in a single night. Needless to say, she was very impressed with the herb and requested a repeat prescription. Two years later, she is still using it successfully.

It was then decided to look at the control of some of the other symptoms; she had also been troubled with ulceration of the stoma site, and this had contributed to the original problem of the ill-fitting ileostomy bags. It was decided to try a tincture that was principally anti-inflammatory in action, but that also contained a number of herbs with marked antibacterial action. Following the first 3-week course of this tincture, the ulcers cleared up and have not reappeared. The patient continues to receive a low maintenance dose of this tincture. Following this improvement, the patient requested help with the recurrent mouth ulcers. A gargle was provided, which effectively controls them; amongst the herbs used were *Commiphora molmol* (myrrh), *Echinacea angustifolia* (cone flower) and *Calendula officinalis* (marigold).

References

Bi-Zhen, W. and Qi-Ying, P. (1988). Functional bowel disorders in apparently healthy Chinese people. *Chinese J. Epid.*, **9**, 345–9.

Bleier, W. (1959). *Zbl. Gynaekol.*, **81**, 701.

Blommaert, K. L. J. and Bartel, E. (1976). Chemotaxonomic aspects of the Buchu species *Agnathosma {Barosma} betulina* and *A. crenulata* from local plantings. *J. S. Afr. Bot.*, **42**, 121–6.

Bommelaer, G., Rouch, M., Dapoigny, M. *et al.* (1986). Epidemiology of intestinal functional disorders in apparently healthy people. *Chin. J. Epid.*., **9**, 345–9.

Cann, P. A., Read, N. W., Holdsworth, C. D. and Barends, D. (1984). Role of loperamide and placebo in management of irritable bowel syndrome. *Dig. Dis. Sci.*, **29**, 239–47.

Chadhuri, K., Torley, H. and Madhok, R. (1997). Cyclosporin. *Br. J. Rheumatol.*, **36**, 1016–21.

Choy, E. H. S. and Scott, D. L. (1997). Drug treatment of rheumatic diseases in the 1990s. *Drugs*, **9**, 183–90.

Conaghan, P.G. and Brooks, P. (1997). Disease-modifying anti-rheumatic drugs. *Curr. Opin. Rheumatol.*, **9**, 183–90.

Cullen, W. (1789). *A Treatise of the Materia Medica*, Vol. 1, p. 431. Edinburgh.

David, T. J. and Cambridge, G. C. (1986). Bacterial infection and atopic eczema. *Arch. Dis. Child.*, **61**, 20–23.

David, T. J. (1987). Steroid scare. *Arch. Dis. Child.*, **62**, 876–8.

David, T. J. (1995). Atopic eczema. *Prescr. J.*, **35(4)**.

Drossman, D. and Thompson, W. G. (1992). The irritable bowel syndrome: review and a graduated multicomponent treatment approach. *Ann. Int. Med.*, **116(12)**, Part 1.

Haller, J. Z. (1961). *Geb. und Gynaekol.*, **56**, 274.

Heaton, K.W. (1994). Irritable bowel syndrome. *Prescr. J.*, **37(4)**.

Heefner, J .D., Wilder, R. M. and Wilson, J. D. (1978). Irritable colon and depression. *Psychosomatics*, **19**, 540–47.

Klein, K. B. (1988). Controlled treatment trials in the irritable bowel syndrome: a critique. *Gastroenterology*, **95**, 232–41.

Kristmundsdottir, F. and David, T. J. (1987). Growth impairment in children with atopic eczema. *J. R. Soc. Med.*, **80**, 9–12.

Kumar, D. and Wingate, D. L. (1985). The irritable bowel syndrome: a paroxysmal motor disorder. *Lancet* **2**, 973–7.

Muller-Ladner, U. (1996). Molecular and cellular interaction in rheumatoid synovium. *Curr. Opin. Rheumatol.*, **8**, 210–20.

O'Dell, J. (1997). Combination DMARD therapy for rheumatoid arthritis: apparent universal acceptance. *Arthr. Rheum.*, **40**(Suppl.) S50.

O'Dell, J., Haire, C. E., Palmer W. *et al.* (1997). Treatment of early rheumatoid arthritis with minocycline or placebo. Results of a randomized double-blind placebo-controlled trial. *Arthr. Rheum.*, **40**, 842–8.

Palmer, K. T. (1992). *Reference Notes for the MRCGP*. Blackwell Science.

Paul, A. A. and Southgate, D. A. T. (1976). *McCance and Widdowson's The Composition of Foods*. HMSO.

Pharmaceutical Journal Practice Checklist (1997). *Irritable Bowel Syndrome*, November 1997.

Probst, V. and Roth, O. A. (1954). On a plant extract with a hormone-like effect. *Deutsch Medizin Zeitschrift*, **79**, 127–34.

Savin, J. A., Paterson, W. D., Adam, K. and Oswald, I. (1979). Effects of trimeprazine and trimipramine on nocturnal scratching in patients with atopic eczema. *Arch. Dermatol.*, **115**, 313–15.

Smart, H. L., Mayberry, J. F. and Atkinson, M. (1986). Alternative medicine consultations and remedies in patients attending a gastroenterology clinic. *Gut*, **27**, 826–8.

Svedlund, J., Sjodin, I., Ottosson, J. O. and Dotevall, G. (1983). Controlled study of psychotherapy in irritable bowel syndrome. *Lancet*, **2**, 589–92.

Walker, E. A., Roy-Byrne, P. P., Katon, W. J. *et al.* (1990). Psychiatric illness and irritable bowel syndrome: a comparison with inflammatory bowel disease. *Am. J. Psych.*, **147**, 1656–61.

Watson, M. C. (1998). Rheumatoid arthritis. *Pharm. J.*, **260**, 310–11.

Weinblatt, M. E. (1996). Methotrexate in rheumatoid arthritis: toxicity issues. *Br. J. Rheumatol.*, **35**, 403–6.

Suggested reading

Burgess, I. (1991). Malathion treatments for headlice – a less reliable treatment than commonly believed. *Pharm. J.*, **247**, 630–32.

Ibarra, J. and Hall, D. (1996). Head lice in schoolchildren. *Arch. Dis. Child.*, **75**, 471–3.

Maskell, R. (1995). Management of recurrent urinary infections in adults. *Prescr. J.*, **35(1)**, 1–11.

Stamm, W. E., Hooton, T. M., Johnson J. R. *et al.* (1989). Urinary tract infections: from pathogenesis to treatment. *J. Infec. Dis.*, **159**, 400–406.

Verhoef, M. J., Sutherland, L. R. and Brkich, L. (1990). Use of alternative medicine by patients attending a gastroenterology clinic. *Can. Med. Assoc. J.*, **142**, 121–5.

10

The herbal management of HIV/AIDS

This chapter will look in detail at the way that patients living with HIV or AIDS (PLWHA) can use herbal medicines as part of their overall management. For the first few years of the epidemic, there was no effective allopathic medication to counter viral activity or boost a failing immune system. AZT (zidovudine, Retrovir) was rediscovered in the mid-1980s, and was found to be effective as single (mono-) therapy for people with advanced disease, though the effect in each individual waned after some months as viral resistance to the drug developed. Results of the Concorde trial in the early 1990s showed that, on its own, it failed to prevent disease progression in asymptomatic people, and it was only in the mid-1990s that the use of combinations of anti-retroviral (anti-HIV) drugs finally produced results. At present these have shown remarkable effects at slowing viral replication, with the consequent improvement in the level of disease severity and in progression rates to AIDS. Viral resistance, however, remains a major problem, leading many patients to fail on current regimes. Part of the reason for this is the difficulty of adherence or compliance to exacting dosage regimes on a life-long basis, and lapses allow viral replication to revive. This increases the likelihood of chance genetic mutation to provide drug-resistance. Consequently, it is not yet known how durable these combination drug regimes will prove in practice.

Herbal medicine was therefore a natural source of help for many patients until these effective drug regimes became established, and it continues to be so for patients suffering ongoing symptomatic disease and, increasingly, side effects of their allopathic medications.

The three main roles

Essentially, there are three roles for herbal medicines in HIV disease; one concerns the search for natural medicines that have anti-retroviral activity, like allopathic antiviral agents. Another addresses the need to maintain the immune system in good shape in order to withstand the onslaught of the virus better, and there has, until very recently, been very little mainstream research activity from the allopathic drug companies in this area. The third role is perhaps the most important and useful, and is the general attention to the overall function of the person. This is true for any chronic illness; the healthier the person overall, the more likely they are to contain the damage done by a particular illness. HIV is certainly no exception to this. I use the word 'person' deliberately, for focusing attention on the functions of the body perpetuates the mind–body separation that characterizes a lot of allopathic intervention. This seems even more the case as medical technology advances; doctors used to be holistic, personal and relatively ineffective, increasingly we are becoming more scientific and impersonal as we achieve greater technological efficacy.

Since the beginning of the epidemic, therefore, allopathic medicine has been trying to attack the virus, while herbal medicine has been trying to boost the specific immune response against it, counteract the side effects of allopathic medication, alleviate the secondary effects of the immune damage itself and, primarily, bring about improved general wellbeing in individuals to allow them to try to live fuller lives as people infected with HIV.

Anti-retroviral effects

In the same way that many plants have innate antibacterial and antiviral substances for their own protection, and are used by herbalists as a type of naturally-occurring antibiotic, so the search has been on for such substances that are active against HIV. The World Health Organization (WHO, 1989) has stimulated this search, and the US National Cancer Institute has screened large numbers of plant extracts *in vitro* (Cardellina *et al.*, 1993). The laboratories at Kew Gardens in London have also been heavily involved. Sometimes this research has been used to increase the repertoire of herbs prescribed by herbalists, and sometimes it has been part of the world-wide push by the pharmaceutical industry to find new allopathic drugs. The epidemic has so far been marked by exciting news of the antiviral effect of this or that plant, and indeed they have been incorporated into herbalists' prescribing with some apparent effect. What has been more difficult has been the attempt to identify and produce an effective isolated constituent, and perhaps this is simply yet another example of the observation that herbal medicines work better when used as the whole plant.

Hypericum perforatum (St. John's wort), for instance, has long been used as an effective antidepressant (see Chapter 8). Hypericin has been thought to be one of the major active constituents. It was found to be active against HIV *in vitro*, and became the focus of some further research. This centres mainly on its inhibition of viral replication from the surface of infected cells, although it may also inhibit reverse transcriptase (in the same way as AZT, etc.) (Meruelo *et al.*, 1988; Degar *et al.*, 1992). Current phase two studies using hypericin itself as an anti-retroviral agent are underway in the developing world. However, in the same way that the whole plant is used effectively for depressive illness, so it is used by herbalists and patients against HIV. Because of the inability to patent the whole plant for this indication, however, few large-scale studies on its action against HIV have so far been conducted. Perhaps the precedent of the New York team's attempt to patent it specifically for its antiviral effect (see Chapter 8) might change this. Smaller studies have shown no effect, but this may well be due to inadequate concentration of the trial medication; the tablets sold over-the-counter usually contain less than 0.15 percent hypericin, whereas liquid extracts and tinctures allow far greater amounts of the active principles to be given.

Castanospermum australe (Australian chestnut or black bean tree), from the Antipodes, has also caused much interest as an anti-retroviral, and studies have so far shown that it inhibits the production of one of the envelope proteins of the virus, preventing binding to human cells (Ruprecht *et al.*, 1989; Fellows and Nash, 1990). Unfortunately, this study uses as its active ingredient castanospermine (a sugar alkaloid), which seems also to cause some malabsorption and weight loss at the effective doses. However, other *in vitro* studies have shown that it acts synergistically with AZT against both main strains of HIV without any increase in toxicity (Johnson *et al.*, 1989). It may also reduce formation of 'syncitia' (the result of fusion of a cell infected with HIV with another that is not) (Walker *et al.*, 1987). The response has been to refine this active agent still further, until it resembles an allopathic anti-retroviral like AZT in both effect and side effects. We are not aware of any trials using the whole plant, to see if effect is maintained without such troublesome side effects.

Momordica charantia (prickly cucumber, bitter melon, or karela) indeed looks like a rather fat cucumber with ridges along it, and is a common sight in the Bangladeshi stores around the health centre in Wapping, where it is sold as a treatment for non-insulin dependent diabetes. It also has a reputation as an antimicrobial agent, including an action against herpes simplex virus. It is blended into a fresh juice, or the water from boiling it is taken orally. Some research shows a variety of relatively potent anti-HIV effects *in vitro*, with corresponding rises in the CD4 count (indicating some restoration of immune function) (Zhang *et al.*, 1992). Minor side effects of diarrhoea and fever have been reported.

'Todoxin' is the working name given to a herbal tincture based on *Taraxacum officinale* (dandelion), with other ingredients so far kept secret by the research teams in the USA and UK. Originating from Yugoslavia, blood samples of patients apparently treated with the medication have been analysed in the UK and show marked reductions in viral load (levels of circulating virus in the peripheral blood of patients with HIV). Current trials are underway in the UK (phase two) and US (randomized and controlled phase three), and interim results are imminently expected.

Curcuma zedoaria (turmeric) provides inhibition of reactivation of latently-infected cells, according to *in vitro* studies, but *in vivo* studies have so far yielded contradictory results (Li *et al.*, 1993; Hellinger *et al.*, 1996). Again, the supposed active agent (curcumin) was used for all these studies, and the authors know of no studies on the whole spice.

Aloe barbadensis (Barbadian aloes) have been shown to reduce HIV replication and syncitium formation in the same way as castanospermine (Kahlon *et al.*, 1991a), and also to act synergistically with AZT (Kahlon *et al.*, 1991b). Again, these studies were conducted on the supposed single active ingredient acemannan.

There are many other references in the literature to plants, and more particularly parts of plants, with exciting anti-retroviral activity. The majority of them are *in vitro* studies, so are difficult to transpose to the clinical situation, and most of them have so far not resulted in significant new allopathic drugs licensed for anti-retroviral use.

It is evident that these attempts to prove or disprove the marked *in vivo* anti-retroviral effect of herbal medicines have not shown important clinical results, although many patients have tried various types and report anecdotal improvement. We would remark that most of the studies are on supposedly active ingredients rather than whole plants, which may well explain the toxicity of some of them. We conclude that using the whole plant may have some relatively minor role to play in reducing viral replication, while minimizing side effects. It may therefore be of more importance used alongside allopathic anti-retroviral drugs in the fight to slow the development of viral resistance, particularly for those taking so-called 'salvage therapy', who have few allopathic options left. However, it would be very unlikely to prove sufficient to prevent HIV disease progression in the vast majority of patients.

Immune modulating effects

This has been an easier role for herbal medicine in the management of patients with HIV, because it fits more naturally into the holistic ethos of herbal medicine – helping the body to help itself. Therefore, the aim of helping the immune system to ward off infection and neoplasia has been generally applied for millennia against all manner of diseases, of which HIV is only the most recent. Herbalists are well trained in this part of the art of medicine, and cognizant of a wide range of such herbs.

Interleukin-2 (IL-2), a naturally occurring immune stimulant (chemokine) produced by the body, was looked at briefly earlier in the epidemic but was found to be relatively ineffective, and indeed probably stimulated HIV replication. Now that effective anti-retrovirals are available it is again being considered, since the former agents are likely to block any increased replication stimulated by the latter. As yet, there is still very little else from allopathic research that looks promising in this area.

Echinacea purpurea (or *E. angustifolia*) has been the main herb in this group throughout the epidemic, having previously been used in a similar way (particularly by the American Indians) to help the immune system ward off other infection, bacterial or viral. Evidence has accumulated quickly over the last decade, mainly from its use in HIV in North America. For once, allopathic pharmacists seem to have been unable to identify particular active ingredients, and the whole plant is used for research, on the assumption that the combination of many ingredients creates the effect. Few side effects from regular use of the tincture have been reported. *In vitro* studies have shown stimulation of macrophages to release tumour necrosis factor, interleukin-1 and beta-interferon. However, many people with HIV already have high levels of some of these, and the effect of further elevating them is uncertain. Indeed, high doses taken regularly may actually decrease immune function (Luettig *et al.*, 1989), and herbalists have therefore often recommended lower or intermittent dosing.

Anxiety about the stimulation of a damaged immune system with Echinacea leading to faster viral replication has led to a general warning that it should be avoided in patients with a CD4 count below 200. An interesting and truly complementary combination of herbal medicine and allopathy has, however, now opened up. The allopathic or hormonal immune modulators (for example, the Interleukin-2 mentioned above) were previously considered to be at least ineffective, if not dangerous, due to the possibility of stimulating viral replication. However, the possibility of simultaneous suppression of this replication using powerful anti-retroviral drugs has allowed trials to start again, using both types of agent, to see if immune system restoration can be speeded up. Perhaps Echinacea could now also have a role here? Many patients are already taking the anti-retrovirals. Why not add some Echinacea in the hope that this will in its own way help to enhance immune recovery?

Astragalus membranaceus is used in Chinese herbal medicine as an immune stimulant, increasing lymphocyte proliferation *in vitro* and reversing immunosuppression in animal experiments (Yan Sun *et al.*, 1983; Da-Tong Che *et al.*, 1998).

Glycyrrhiza glabra (liquorice) is again a Chinese herb, but is also well known in the West. It, too, seems to have immune stimulant properties as well as antiviral ones, in particular the blocking of cell-to-cell transmission of HIV (Ito *et al.*, 1987; Akamatsu, 1991; Hirabayashi *et al.*, 1991).

Eleutherococcus senticosus (Siberian ginseng), not to be confused with the unrelated Korean ginseng (*Panax ginseng*), may stimulate the activity of both CD4 and CD8 (killer) lymphocytes (Shechezhin *et al.*, 1977), and its legendary role as an anabolic agent for body-builders may be an allied effect.

Aloe barbadensis (already mentioned above for its anti-retroviral activity) also seems to possess the potential to modulate the immune system separately (McDaniel *et al.*, 1987). Aqueous extracts of *Pinus parviflora* (Japanese White Pine cones) may induce human T cell lines to reduce HIV replication, possibly by a low molecular weight protein that bears little resemblance to naturally-occurring human cytokines (Tamura *et al.*, 1991).

These herbs are not native to Western Europe, however, and herbal traditions from around the world stress the preference for the use of local plants. We don't yet know how scientific this is, and many younger herbalists and naturopaths are keen to experiment with this cross-cultural interplay. However, the reputation of plants is dependent on the context in which they have been used for many centuries, and it is therefore often difficult to splice a foreign herb into a more local medical system.

Overall function of the person

Help with the secondary effects of HIV infection

Moving into the area of the opportunistic infections, tumours and reactive conditions that characterize the symptomatology of someone with more advanced HIV disease, herbal medicine perhaps has more to offer. Many of these conditions are seen much more commonly in HIV-negative patients, so herbalists have more experience in dealing with them. The conditions can generally also be dealt with in the same way, although of course they may be more severe and require simultaneous allopathic therapy. Examples include eczema or dry skin, psoriasis, folliculitis, seborrhoeic dermatitis, asthma, recurrent chest or gut infections, oral thrush, lymphadeno-pathy, night sweats, fatigue, anorexia, insomnia, anxiety and depression. It would be rare for the majority of these to be so severe that any delay introduced by the ministrations of a herbalist would be in any way dangerous; however, it would be incumbent upon the herbalist to be aware of the so-called 'red flag' conditions such as *Pneumocystis carinii* pneumonia when dealing with a patient with HIV. Indeed, perhaps the majority of symptoms and conditions in this list are relatively resistant to most allopathic intervention, and may well respond better to the use of herbal medicine and its accompanying dietary and lifestyle advice.

Improved general wellbeing

Galium aparine is indicated for lymphadenopathy, and as a general tonic for the nervous system. Commonly known as goose grass or cleavers, this is the pleasant nuisance often experienced on cross-country walks in summer, when its long stems cling to our clothes. It is less specifically an immune stimulant, but moves us more into the arena where herbal medicine perhaps has the most part to play in the management of patients with HIV; a general improvement in the vitality of the organs of the body, helping them to function more efficiently.

HIV disease has marked similarities to ageing: increased organ failure, neoplasia, degenerative diseases, and the inability to deal with the waste products of metabolism. Linked with the effects of prolonged and aggressive allopathic therapy, there is a need for agents that help to maintain good organ function and clear the effects of the build up of catabolic products. *Galium aparine* is only one of the many herbs that fall into this category. *Taraxacum officinale* (dandelion) and *Silybum marianum* (milk or holy thistle) are two others, and have a more specific cleansing effect on the liver, allowing it to maintain its important role in clearing drugs and catabolic products at a steady rate. It is here that the herbalist feels more at home; dealing with the effects of HIV disease in much the same way as with the similar effects of many other chronic and degenerative diseases. Consequently, a thorough knowledge of HIV infection is not a *sine qua non* for herbalists, in the same way that GPs are perfectly well able to deal with patients with HIV from first principles and the intuition gained from experience, so long as there is also an awareness of the spectrum of more serious clinical manifestation to allow for specialist discussion or onward referral. The existence of a medical herbalist alongside primary (or even secondary) care teams may therefore permit useful exploration of the possibilities of gentle immune stimulation and anti-retroviral assistance, and bolstering of the vital strength of the individual to cope with the medical, physical and psychosocial stresses common in HIV or AIDS.

References

Akamatsu, H. (1991). Mechanism of anti-inflammatory action of Glycyrrhizin: effect on neutrophil functions, including reactive species generation. *Planta Medica*, **57**, 119–21.

Cardellina, J., Gustafson, K., Beutler, J. *et al.* (1993). National Cancer Institute intramural research on human immunodeficiency virus and anti-tumor plant natural products. In *Human Medicinal Agents from Plants*, ACS Symposium Series 534 (A. Kinghorn and M. Balandrin, eds). American Chemical Society.

Da-Tong Chu *et al.* (1998). Immunotherapy with Chinese medicinal herbs. II. Reversal of cyclophosphamide-induced immune suppression by administration of fractionated *Astragalus membranaceus in vivo. J. Clin. Lab. Immunol.*, **25**, 125–9.

Degar, S. *et al.* (1992). Inactivation of the human immunodeficiency virus by hypericin: evidence for photochemical alterations of p24 and a block in uncoating. *AIDS Res. Hum. Retro.*, **8(11)**, 1929–36.

Fellows, L. and Nash, R. (1990). Sugar-shaped alkaloids. *Sci. Progr. Oxford*, **74**, 245–55.

Hellinger, J. A. *et al.* (1996). Phase I/II randomized, open-label study of oral curcumin safety, and antiviral effects on HIV-RT PCR in HIV+ individuals. *Abstract 140, 3rd Conf. Retro. Opp. Inf.*, Washington.

Hirabayashi, K. *et al.* (1991). Antiviral activities of Glycyrrhizin and its modified compounds against human immunodeficiency type 1 and herpes simplex virus *in vitro*. *Chem. Pharm. Bull.*, **39(1)**, 112–15.

Ito, M. *et al.* (1987). Inhibitory effect of Glycyrrhizin on the *in vitro* infectivity and cytopathic activity of the human immunodeficiency virus (HIV). *Antiviral Res.*, **7**, 127–37.

Johnson, V., Walker, B., Barlow, M. *et al.* (1989). Synergistic inhibition of human immunodeficiency virus type 1 and type 2 replication *in vitro* by castanospermine and 3-azido-3-deoxythymidine. *Antimic Agents Chemother.*, **33**, 53–7.

Kahlon, J., Kemp, M., Yawei, N. *et al.* (1991). Inhibition of AIDS virus replication by acemannan *in vitro*. *Mol. Biother.*, **3**, 127–35.

Kahlon, J., Kemp, M., Yawei, N. *et al.* (1991). *In vitro* evaluation of the synergistic antiviral effects of acemannan in combination with azidothymidine and acyclovir. *Mol. Biother.*, **3**, 214–23.

Li, C. J. *et al.* (1993). Three inhibitors of type 1 immunodeficiency virus long terminal repeat-directed gene expression and virus replication. *PNAS*, **90**, 1839–42.

Luettig, B. *et al.* (1989). Macrophage activation by the polysaccharide arabinogalactan isolated from plant cell cultures of *Echinacea purpurea. J. Natl. Cancer Inst.,* **89,** 669.

McDaniel, H., Perkins, S. and McAnalley, B. (1987). A clinical pilot using Carrisyn in the treatment of acquired immunodeficiency syndrome (AIDS). *Am. J. Clin. Pathol.,* **88, 5**34.

Meruelo, D., Lavie, G. and Kavie, D. (1988). Therapeutic agents with dramatic antiretroviral activity and little toxicity at effective doses: aromatic polycyclic diones hypericin and pseudohypericin. *Proc. Acad. Natl. Sci. USA,* **85,** 5230–34.

Ruprecht, R. M. *et al.* (1989). *In vivo* analysis of castanospermine, a candidate antiretroviral agent. *J. AIDS,* **2,** 149–157.

Shechezhin, A. K. *et al.* (1977). Tentative data on the mass Eleutherococcus prophylaxis of influenza at the main assembly line and metallurgical plant of the Volga Automobile plant. *2nd All-Union Conf. Adapt. Man.*

Tamura, Y., Lai, P., Bradley, W. *et al.* (1991). A soluble factor induced by an extract from *Pinus parviflora* Sieb. Et Zucc. can inhibit the replication of human immunodeficiency virus *in vitro. Proc. Natl. Acad. Sci. USA,* **88,** 2249–53.

Walker, B., Kowalski, M., Goh, W. *et al.* (1987). Inhibition of human immunodeficiency virus syncitium formation and virus replication by castanospermine. *Proc. Natl. Acad. Sci. USA,* **84,** 8120–24.

World Health Organization (1989). *In vitro* screening of traditional medicines for anti-HIV activity. Memorandum from a World Health Organization Meeting. *Bull WHO,* **67,** 613–18.

Yan Sun *et al.* (1983). Preliminary observations on the effects of the Chinese medicinal herbs *Astragalus membranaceus* and *Ligustrum lucidum* on lymphocyte blastogenic responses. *J. Biol. Resp. Modifiers,* **2,** 227–37.

Zhang, Q. C. *et al.* (1992). Primary report on the clinical use of Chinese herbal extract of *Momordica charantia* (bitter melon) in HIV-infected patients. *Abstract PuB 7597, 8th Intl. Conf. AIDS,* Amsterdam.

Suggested reading

AIDS Treatment Directory (1998). NAM Publications.

Wright, C. W. (1995). Natural products in the fight against AIDS. *Pharm. J.,* **254,** 583–7.

11

The GP and the herbalist: a working symbiosis

Complementary therapists have consistently been sidelined from allopathic (western or orthodox) medicine in the UK, not only through official and financial exclusion from the NHS, but also through physical separation from it. The Health Service continues on its allopathic way within subsidized health centres, GP surgeries and hospitals, while other healthcare professionals have to find and fund their own premises themselves. Frequently they work in groups with therapists from other complementary disciplines, in an unsubsidized equivalent of a health centre, with receptionists, waiting areas and separate consulting rooms. All prescribing has to be paid for at full cost, and access to clinical investigations (blood tests, radiographs, etc.) is both difficult and expensive. Referrals to allopathic specialists are not usually possible without prior referral to the patient's general practitioner, who may well decide that such a referral is not indicated and be generally unwilling to trust such a therapist with whom he or she has no professional relationship. There is no equivalent or parallel system of complementary 'consultant specialists', so the therapist is often left to practise alone without any recourse to a second opinion, unless the patient is referred on to a known colleague with a special interest. There is rarely any of the on-site back-up seen in modern allopathic NHS primary care teams (practice nursing, health visiting, psychology or counselling, community midwifery), which provides such useful multidisciplinary interaction, discussion, and management of many patients nowadays.

The case for mainstream complementary therapy having its routine base within allopathic health centres and primary healthcare teams therefore seems an easy one to make. By way of example, let's look again at the example of the medical herbalist based at Wapping Health Centre in the East End of London. This is an NHS-owned health centre with a full primary care team, including GPs, practice and health promotion nurses, receptionists and practice/health centre manager, district nurses, health visitors, school nurses, dentist, community midwives and a visiting paediatrician. There is even a hearing-aid technician who visits once a month, not to mention the hoards of medical, nursing, and other students passing through.

Now there is also a medical herbalist on the team once a week, for a full day's consultations, bookable by self-referral or via one of the other health-workers through the fully staffed reception desk.

The consultation

Patients are usually familiar with the layout of the centre and with the reception staff, and are therefore more likely to feel at ease. They are seen in a consulting room that they may well recognize, with its familiar allopathic paraphernalia of travel vaccination posters, FP10 prescription pads, investigation request forms, needles and syringes. A medical student may be sitting in to observe the consultation. It's just like attending any other healthcare appointment.

The herbalist starts with an introduction and series of questions which, although more detailed than usual (for she has more time to offer), seem logical and comprehensible. All the facilities are available for a full clinical examination.

A medical, personal and social history takes a shape familiar to any allopathic practitioner, and is written in a separate set of notes, though often with a brief summary in the main Lloyd-George folder or on the networked computer patient record.

The herbalist may well have a written referral note from the patient's GP or practice nurse. The patient's own notes will have been available for the herbalist to look at in advance or for checking something during the course of the consultation. The herbalist knows the patient's GP well, having met regularly in the corridor and tea-room and at meetings many times over the last few years, and may well have discussed the case personally before the initial appointment.

Patient management and prescribing

Finally the herbalist explains the underlying problem to the patient, wholly from a herbalist's perspective, and suggests how the condition could be managed. This might involve arranging for the practice nurse to take some blood, sometimes right after the consultation, or agreeing to discuss the need for an X-ray with the patient's GP, or even a consultant referral for further investigation or advice — perhaps to exclude a potentially serious diagnosis that might require allopathic treatment. The idea behind any herbal medicines that might be prescribed is explained, and the FP10 that will be signed by the GP is issued. The patient can then take it to one of the local chemists for dispensing. Many patients in this part of inner London are exempt from charges for their medicines, and will be able to receive their herbal medicines free of charge. Those who do pay generally suffer only a single item charge, as the herbal medicine is usually a mixture of several plant tinctures in one bottle (though occasionally a powder, tablet or cream are also prescribed). The local chemists understand these formulations; indeed, they bear close resemblance to the ones they learned at college, and provide a pleasant – if sometimes time-consuming – alternative to handing out boxes of pills. The Health Authority long ago agreed to honour these prescriptions, in the same way that it does for homoeopathic ones, which are often written by GPs with a special interest. The GPs have agreed that the herbalist can prescribe any of the herbal medicines that are normally used and are unlikely to have side effects or interactions with any allopathic drugs. These prescriptions are then automatically signed by the patient's GP.

Schedule Three medicines (herbal medicines that fall under this section of the Medicines Act 1968) are dealt with separately. These medicines have a more profound physiological effect, and so are potentially more dangerous, and with more interactions with other allopathic drugs that the patient might be taking. Examples include *Atropa belladonna* (deadly nightshade), which contains atropine, and *Ephedra sinica* (Ma Huang), which contains ephedrine. These are issued as separate private prescriptions, and are dispensed from the herbalist's own private dispensary. This transfers any responsibility for these medications from the GPs to the herbalist, and to the herbalist's own professional indemnity, which works in the same way as for registered doctors. Further, the herbalist marks the patient's written record with this prescription and its general mode of action ('adrenergic' or 'anticholinergic', etc.), thereby alerting the GPs to any likely interactions with drugs that they may subsequently wish to prescribe. The computer record may also be marked in the same fashion, leaving a warning on the prescribing page that an allopathically-active herbal medicine has been prescribed, and that care should be taken before prescribing anything similar or interactive. It is usually possible for the computer database to have added to it the (short) list of such herbal medications, so that they will appear as one item in the standard acute or repeat list of the patient's medications. The database asks for a therapeutic group to be attributed to each new item, so *Atropa belladonna* would be included in the 'anticholinergic' group. Anyone subsequently trying to prescribe something similar, or interacting, would then trigger the usual on-screen computer warning.

In fact, the herbalist very rarely uses this type of medication, both because it will effectively have been tried before in allopathic form (as an extraction of the 'active ingredient'), and also because this is not the principal mode of action of herbal medicine. Problems of prescribing, whether interactions with allopathic medications or side effects to be dealt with in the herbalist's absence, are therefore rare. The herbalist's ready availability on the telephone to both patients and primary care staff provides further back-up and advice where necessary.

The patient leaves the consultation armed with a diet diary, arranging a follow-up appointment for a couple of weeks or so. The diary allows the herbalist to see if the patient's food intake already constitutes some form of herbal medicine, and the potential for the diet to improve his or her condition. An example of this might be the injunction to 'eat a bowl of porridge a day'. Many herbalists that I trained with have found this to be an easy and non-medical way of getting a patient to take an effective daily dose of *Avena sativa* (oats), widely used as a 'trophorestorative' (an agent that helps to restore the balance of the patient's mental health, frequently in the direction of antidepression). Coupled with *Hypericum perforatum* (St. John's wort) this might well form the basis of a good prescription for mild depression, malaise or fatigue. Knowing the quantity of oats already included in the patient's diet (in other cereal mixtures for breakfast, biscuits or otherwise) is therefore important information, and provides a very patient-friendly way of tailoring the intervention to existing dietary habits. Similarly, there are other occasions when it would be part of the management of a patient's condition to know about, and perhaps modify, the intake of other 'medically active' dietary ingredients such as garlic, horseradish, parsley, celery … The list is long.

How to pay for the herbalist's services

There is no fee payable by the patient, the herbalist's time currently being paid for by the Prescribing Incentive Scheme, whereby the GPs' prescribing is within certain notional budget limits and according to certain agreed guidelines. This scheme provides money, not for the GPs personally, but for improvements to patient care at the surgery, and can mean anything from new chairs in the waiting room to new diagnostic or therapeutic equipment, or payments for ancillary medical staff. This Health Authority is happy to include the medical herbalist. The scheme may change soon with the advent of locality commissioning through the new Primary Care Groups, which will allow local GPs to decide whether such attachments would provide cost-efficiencies to patient management across the district or widen and improve existing health service provision. The herbalist at Wapping is able to show a considerable lightening of the clinical burden, especially with the so-called 'heartsink patients'. These patients consult all the primary care team frequently and for long appointments with conditions that do not easily fall into the allopathic diagnostic or therapeutic arena; however, the longer consultation with the herbalist may provide more successful lifestyle and dietary advice, and more patient-friendly herbal medicine management. GP-referrals for costly investigations or consultant opinions – sometimes out of desperation at what to do next – may also be considerably reduced, without trying to 'fob the patient off' with inaction or prescribing placebo medication.

Interaction with the rest of the team

When there is an appropriate opportunity, or at the next monthly meeting with the GPs and practice nurses, the patient's condition is discussed and the herbalist puts forward his or her view of it. The similarity in medical history taking and examination allows an easier understanding of one another's previous or planned problem solving, and the herbalist can explain the management of the patient's condition. Subsequent meetings will allow feedback of the patient's progress, further discussion and plans for discharge. A more detailed summary is often written for the Lloyd-George file or computer record.

Gradually, as the months and years go by, the number of referrals is steadily rising, and the other members of the primary healthcare team are becoming increasingly glad of the in-house availability of someone who relishes trying to sort out some of their 'heartsink patients'. This unfortunate term is often (rather offensively) applied to patients who consult their GPs and other members of the team frequently with problems that are not easy to define or sort out within the normal western medical ('biomedical') tradition. We know that as many as 50 per cent of consultations may relate to the presentation of a symptom-picture by the patient that does not end with the attachment of a recognizably biomedical diagnostic label. Some definitions have even used the thickness of the medical record as an indicator of 'heartsink patients', anything more than a couple of centimetres thick leading to a more-or-less audible sigh from the doctor on seeing the set of notes for the surgery ahead.

A spiral often develops, with increasing patient exasperation with the inadequacies of their medical management matched by increasingly automatic dismissal by the GP of all symptoms as being spurious, or not grounded in any 'real' medical problems. Alternatively, GPs may feel increasingly powerless to help someone who continues to come with a variety of problems that they cannot solve. This has been explained by the difference between 'illness' and 'disease', where the former is the subjective experience of the patient and usually involves areas not encompassed by the narrower biomedical definition of the latter, which looks primarily at pathological dysfunction of part of the body. The less narrowly-defined and less biomedical tradition of herbal medicine allows the difference between illness and disease to be more easily bridged, so patients may well feel that their overall experience of illness is more readily understood and taken into consideration when their management is discussed. At the same time, patients are able to feel that there is discussion between the herbalist and the other members of the primary healthcare team, so the benefits of both approaches are more likely to come together in a synergistic whole. This set-up also avoids the 'covering-up' that patients frequently resort to, feeling embarrassed about admitting to their GPs that they have been to seek advice from a complementary therapist. It is likely therefore that many 'heartsink patients' will benefit from input from a variety of sources of help, and that the addition of someone less reductionist to the primary healthcare team may well help them to experience less intense 'illness', with a consequent fall in attendance and dependence on their GPs alone.

The herbalist may also sometimes do some home visits during the lunch hour, particularly to the frail, housebound elderly or to patients housebound with AIDS, or to the residents of an old peoples' home cared for by the practice. In its limited way, this may help to reduce the number of routine home visits done by other members of the team.

Gradually, the GPs and nurses may begin to understand some of the commoner plant medicines, perhaps prescribing some of the simpler ones themselves during their own consultations or, better still, trying them out for their own or their families' ailments at home.

The herbalist's patients seem to take warmly to the increased time, attention and lack of allopathic medication, and hence the herbalist's DNA ('did-not-attend') rate is very low. Similarly, the herbalist enjoys trying to achieve success where others have failed, as this not only helps patients and GPs or practice nurses alike, but demonstrates the efficacy of this approach to therapy. Care is taken not to belittle the allopathic approach of colleagues at the Health

Centre, yet the herbalist is able to offer an alternative way for patients who feel that they have not benefited from it. Often the health visitor will bypass the GP altogether – for a baby with eczema, for instance – referring the mother directly for more effective and safer herbal medicine (usually as a cream).

The herbalist's awareness of allopathic medications, which is part of the training, allows a good idea of any of their possible side effects, and also of any possible interactions with herbal preparations. Thus, herbal medicine can sometimes be used to help alleviate some of the side effects of the patient's allopathic drugs, or may slowly assist in improving the underlying condition, so that the dose of the drugs can gradually be reduced – by the GP, not the herbalist – and maybe eventually even discontinued.

The GP's conclusion

The presence of a fully trained and experienced medical herbalist in the practice has allowed a widening of the healthcare base to patients. It has taken up some of the burden of 'heartsink' patients, introduced an interesting and useful dimension to the practice of other primary healthcare staff, and reduced the need for expensive allopathic medication or consultant referral. With the advent of an increasingly primary care led NHS, all these features could become increasingly valuable, and can only help to begin reducing the mistrust and ignorance that still exists between allopathic and complementary medicine in the UK.

Appendix 1

Tinctures prepared from organically grown herbs can be obtained from:

Granary Herbs
The Granary
Milgate Park
Bearsted
Kent ME14 4NN.

Information on all aspects of training in herbal medicine can be obtained from:

The National Institute of Medical Herbalists
56 Longbrook Street
Exeter
Devon EX4 6AH.

Appendix 2

NAME

Age if under 12 years	
yrs.	mths.

Address

Pharmacy Stamp

Pharmacist's pack & quantity endorsement	No. of days treatment N.B. Ensure dose is stated	**NP**		*Pricing Office use only*

TINCTURE

Viburnum opulus   3

Filipendula u'ia a   20

Altn.. oppicn lis (RADIX)   20

Glycyrrhiza glabra F.E   10

Matricaria recutita   20
_____
100

(200)   5ml tds

Signature of Doctor | Date

For pharmacist No. of Prescns. on form

IMPORTANT:- Read the notes overleaf before going to the pharmacy

An example of a herbal prescription.

Index